The Moms' Club Diaries

The Moms' Club Diaries

Notes from a World of Play Dates, Pacifiers, and Poignant Moments

Compiled by Allyson Condie
and Lindsay Hepworth

spring creek
BOOK COMPANY
Provo, Utah

ISBN: 978-1-932898-92-7
e. 1

Published by:
Spring Creek Book Company
P.O. Box 50355
Provo, Utah 84605-0355

www.springcreekbooks.com

Cover design by Nicole Cunningham
Cover design © Spring Creek Book Company

Printed in the United States of America
10 9 8 7 6 5 4 3 2 1
Printed on acid-free paper

Library of Congress Cataloging-in-Publication Data

The moms' club diaries : notes from a world of play dates, pacifiers, and poignant
moments / compiled by Allyson Condie and Lindsay Hepworth.
     p. cm.
  ISBN 978-1-932898-92-7 (pbk. : alk. paper)
  1. Mothers--Case studies. 2. Mothers--Conduct of life. 3. Motherhood. 4. Women--
Case studies. I. Condie, Allyson Braithwaite. II. Hepworth, Lindsay.

HQ759.M847 2008
306.874'30882893--dc22
                                    2008000580

Dedication

For Emily Parkinson Dunford
Who mothers with grace and humor
And who is not afraid of hard things

Table of Contents

Introduction

by Allyson Condie

This book came about because of a question. It's a question I never encountered as a high school student, a college student, or when I was working as a teacher. But, ever since I became a stay-at-home mom, it's a question I've heard with great frequency:

"What do you *do* all day?"

I could tell them the short version: I took care of two toddlers.

I could tell them the long version. We got up. We got dressed. We ate breakfast and made sure everyone was clean and dry. Doing those four things took two hours, and then it was time for the one-year-old's morning nap. I wrangled him to bed and tried to clean up the house from the morning's activities and simultaneously entertain the three-year-old, who seemed to have decided that it would be a good idea to get out his play dough and separate it into infinitesimal pieces so small they had to be vacuumed up, to his great distress (which increased when I took away the pieces he had slated for human consumption). Then I added insult to injury and made him go to the potty, since it was obvious it had to happen, even though we are out of potty treats (otherwise known as fruit snacks).

In desperation, I ransacked the Halloween candy that I

had bought early on sale and was saving for Halloween night. I opened a tiny yellow box of those sticky Dots that I remember from going to the movies when I was young. I cut one Dot in half and gave it to him for his treat, and ate the rest of the box myself on the sly. And I didn't eat it piece by piece as the morning went along. No, I shoved the other six Dots into my mouth and almost cemented my jaw together, and I had to turn my head or hide my mouth behind my hand while he asked me questions and I gummed through my illicit snack. That gets us to approximately 9 a.m., which is when the one-year-old's morning nap came to an early and ignominious end when he woke up in need of a diaper change.

I don't think they want the long version.

In talking with other mothers of young children, I have found that I am certainly not alone in being asked this question. There are many of us out there, many of us who have humorous and tragic and happy and heartbreaking and noisy and quiet stories to tell of what we do all day. These networks of other mothers, of women, friends, and sisters, are part of what keep us all afloat.

Mothering young children is intense. It's physically intense, a daily marathon of small motions (cutting toast into squares, bending and lifting a toddler) and large ones (chasing kids through the park, pushing strollers uphill for miles when the car breaks down). It's mentally intense (keeping yourself intellectually alive while reading the same stories over and over; learning about things as varied as nursing babies, identifying illnesses, and teaching children to read). And it's spiritually intense. Teaching your little ones while trying to keep your own spirituality afloat can be one of the hardest parts of motherhood. It's a lot for one person to do.

That's where other moms come in.

We're all in this together, and we hope that, in sharing our embarrassments and missteps and the lessons we've had to learn over and over again, we can also share some of the love and tenderness and growth that we have experienced in the refiner's fire that is motherhood. We don't have all the answers, and we're not perfect moms. We simply want to share our stories in case they help.

This is a collection of experiences and essays from other Latter-day Saint mothers who have also been asked what, exactly, they do all day. The answers are different, but the motivation is the same. Love. We love our children, we love the gospel, and we love the Savior and have learned time and time again that he never meant for us to do this alone.

This is what we do all day.

I Didn't Think This Through

by Allyson Condie

When I was a teenager, and working very hard to be cool, I would sometimes catch myself humming aloud the music my dad listened to in his car on our way to school. Walking down the halls, or running in a race, I would catch myself singing bits of Simon and Garfunkel and Bruce Springsteen and Neil Diamond. I couldn't get them out of my mind—they were imbedded there, against my will.

Now that I'm a mom, there are a few litanies that repeat over and over in my head, unbidden. "Don't forget the diapers. Put him to sleep on his back. The car seat straps should fit snugly, with the top buckle at armpit level."

The one that I seem to hear the most is, "I didn't think this through."

I thought it when I was about to deliver my first child via an emergency c-section, and I looked around the room full of people I didn't know who now had our lives in their hands. Few of them spoke English as a first language, and my husband was wearing an elastic shower cap and doing his best to look reassuring, but only succeeding in looking young and scared.

1

I thought it when we were the house parents for a sorority, and I heaved my eight months pregnant body out the door one morning to get the mail, while wearing my pajamas. The frat boys who had just arrived to play a prank looked at me in what can only be described as unadulterated horror. "Hi!" I said, and they literally ran.

Don't get me wrong. At no point have I ever regretted having my children. I've just regretted my own inability to see far enough ahead. I always pictured my children as snuggly babies, and I also pictured them at random other intervals in their lives, shrouded in picturesque haze: as eight year olds, walking into the waters of baptism; as teenagers, running around a track or playing soccer; going on missions; getting married.

It's only now that I recognize the level of trust and faith that go into each of those large endeavors, and into the little endeavors that also come along the way. I never thought I'd be a clingy, neurotic parent; I still don't want to be. But I didn't think this through. I didn't think through the hundred little ways they grow away from you through your life, and how that will ache a little, or a lot.

I want them to experience life and missions and school and marriage and being parents. I do want that for them. But is it too much to ask that nothing bad ever happen to them, or that I be able to come along every step of the way?

My oldest son endured several surgeries and many procedures in the first few years of his life. We were lucky; the outcome was positive, and what we went through was not comparable to what many other parents endure for much longer. But there were many times when I sat and held his hand as he cried and realized that I had not thought this through. I had imagined the happiness I would give him—the fun days at the park. I had not fully realized that, in giving him the joy of life, I was also giving him the possibility of pain. A lot of pain, in fact. Pain that I hadn't predicted, pain that I couldn't control, and pain that I couldn't take away from him. I hadn't anticipated putting him into the hands of someone else, a doctor, and watching him go down the hall, wearing a tiny hospital gown. And even if I had pictured the pain, I could never have known what it would feel like until I went through it with the actual little person I loved so much. You can't think that through. You only *feel* it through, when it actually happens.

I also hadn't thought through the idea of preschool fully. I did pretty well on the first day of preschool—I missed him, but I trusted his teacher, and it felt good to give his little brother some one-on-one time (something else I hadn't thought through—the guilt of not being able to spend as much time with each child as you did with the one before).

But, even though the first day went well, Special Day did not. Special Day was something to which I had looked forward, because it was the day I got to be the parent helper in the classroom and see what his new little world was all about.

But, as always, I hadn't thought it through, even though I truly had prepared. He was wearing clean clothes, his face had been washed, his cowlick had been temporarily subdued, and he had a special item to share during Circle Time (his stuffed tiger, Hobbes). I had arranged babysitting for his fabulously adorable little brother. I had the snacks prepared and ready to go. And, not only had I showered, but I was also wearing a little makeup. It promised to be a red-letter day for both of us.

It turned out that my preschooler was not as interested in spending the day with me as I was in spending it with him. I thought it would be fun if I hung out near him while he played trains with his friends during Choice Time. He did not. He suggested that I play something else, with someone else. Luckily, the girls seemed to like me. We built a big house for the stuffed animals out of blocks and I pretended to be Mommy Cat. Mommy Cat was, for the most part, very purry and attentive. She did keep sneaking peeks at the little brown-haired boy in the gray basketball sweatshirt and telling herself that he didn't need her simply because he was so well-adjusted. This was actually a good sign, Mommy Cat decided—a sign of independence and security.

Feeling better, I got out the milk, apples, and graham crackers that my son had chosen to bring for Snack Time. "Snack Time!" sang Miss Mary, the teacher, and they all washed their hands and popped into their seats. My little guy sat next to some of the other kids and beamed up at me. His cowlick had sprouted again from the back of his head. I poured his milk first. I couldn't help it.

"Where did this milk come from?" asked an adorable, cherubic, blond-curled little boy as I poured him a glass.

"From cows," I told him, smiling.

He burst out laughing. "Milk doesn't come from cows! Milk comes from crushed-up soybeans!"

"Some milk does," I said, getting the slightest bit defensive. "*Some* milk comes from cows."

He kept giggling, and soon everyone had joined it. "Milk doesn't come from cows!" they giggled to one another. Even my preschooler, who always drinks milk that comes from cows, and who wouldn't know a soybean if it came to life and introduced itself, joined in.

I don't know why it hurts your self-esteem to have fifteen little four-year-olds looking up and laughing at you, but it kind of does. "Ha ha!" I said, pouring more milk for all of them, trying to laugh too, realizing that preschool was a different world, a world where, to my little boy, it wasn't the Mommy-and-Me show at all. I suppose this should have been obvious. Still, it was the first hallmark of his growing away from me, and it hurt a little. I found myself feeling a little lonely as I walked around pouring the milk while he laughed and talked with his friends.

For most of his short little life, it had been the two of us together all day. Even now, with six hours of preschool per week factored in, we are together most of the time. We eat every meal together. He wakes me up in the morning. We brush our teeth together, pick up toys together, go to the store and the doctor and the dentist together. When his little brother came along, he became an indispensable part of the group, another comrade in the club. Although sometimes I feel like all I do is help other people eat and have naps and go to the bathroom (while never getting to do any of those things myself), I have two little friends who are always with me. I have two happy little tour guides to life. They point out things, like buses, that I don't notice without them. They sing me songs. Sometimes, they think I am hilarious, when I say things like, "See you later, alligator."

After the snack, I did get to help him put on his boots and hat for Outside Time, but that was it. During Outside Time, he wanted to run and chase John, another parent who was helping that day, with all the other boys. I sat in the little wooden bus and read stories to some kids who had brought books out with them, glancing over to where my little boy ran happily around in the biting winter air, without a care in the world, without me.

After Special Day was over, we went home to our cute little brother/son, and had lunch and played and did naps and played some more and folded laundry (me) and jumped on and unfolded laundry (the boys) and made dinner and did bath time and went to bed. And I forgot about Special Day in the busyness of the rest of Regular Day, and he wanted me to play with him and color with him and he said "I love you" at least three or four times.

But at night, Special Day came back to haunt me. That always happens at night, after saying that prayer and climbing into bed. Before I had kids, I thought about lots of different things while I waited for sleep to find me. Now, I almost always think about one thing: my children. I ask myself questions. Did I love them? Yes. Did I tell them that? Yes. Did I show them? Yes, by making their sandwiches and changing their diapers and locating their turtle backpacks and finding it impossible to resist kissing their soft little cheeks.

But what tears me up inside after they are in bed, when I've had a few minutes to myself, is how imperfectly I've loved them. Often, I want to wake them up and try again.

As a mother, or at least, if you are this mother, you fail them a hundred little ways every day. When the baby spat out his pacifier and then demanded it again immediately, I only rinsed it. When my preschooler wanted to say the blessing at lunch and then was silly about it, I said it myself after he was finished to save time, and didn't give him another chance. I remember other mistakes, the big ones, the time I drove to the store and realized that I had never actually buckled the baby into his car seat. I felt like driving straight to Social Services and turning myself in for being negligent. (Where were my unbidden litanies then, when I really needed them to remind me about carseat safety? Due to a short-circuit in my mind, I was probably humming "America" to myself instead.)

The night after Special Day, I thought of a myriad of ways I'd failed. They ran the gamut from little things (maybe I should have brought soy milk instead?) to big (I should be more crazy and playful like John, the other parent visiting) to cosmic guilt (Why am I such an imperfect parent?) to colossal dread about the future (He's only going to grow farther and farther away from me, and I can't stand it). And I realize that I haven't thought this through on so many levels. I ask myself again: Is it too much to ask that nothing bad ever happen to them, or that I be able to come along every step of the way?

And I realize that it is.

There's only one thing to be done. It's called Second Prayer (in keeping with the titles of Special Day). That's when I get back out of bed again and pray again, a second time, asking for help to do better the next day, to have more faith, to trust more that all of this is going to turn out beautifully someday. More patience, more faith, more trust.

I've found that the lessons I've had about unselfishness and patience and faith and holding on and letting go are ones I have to learn again, every single day. Luckily, the one about unconditional love is not. And, blessedly, there is someone there who is willing to listen to Second, and Third, and Hundredth Prayer, all through the years, and who *has* thought this through, every step of it.

Traveling

by Amy Ferguson Hackworth

My small town eyes were always wide open to the busy city, the history, and the culture of London during the semester I spent there as a student. For me, the best part was meeting people. I glibly started conversations in the park and interrupted reading commuters on the train to hear a British accent and a story about a person's day. It was even better when someone started a conversation with me. On Easter Sunday I walked a flower-lined path in Kensington Gardens when a disheveled old man approached me. Blue eyes looked out from under a plaid cap. He wore an oxford shirt and a scarf and at least two cardigan sweaters under his coat. "Are you a traveler?" he asked. I liked the philosophical implications of the question—not just that I was away from home, but that I was a traveler, the sort to seek adventure and explore.

"I am traveling," I answered, and we talked about the value of seeing new things. "So many people walk around blind," he said. Gesturing toward a gigantic tree, he asked, "What is that object?"

"A tree," I answered confidently.

"Ah, yes, a tree. You see a tree and then walk past, ignoring its remarkable details. The minute you call it a tree, you lose its shape, its forms. You name it and forget about it," he accused. "Look at the majestic trunk, the gnarled branches, the immense detail. It's a masterpiece. But you call it a tree, and keep walking."

Years later I travel a decidedly different path. After breakfast this morning I realize we are out of milk and bread and I am having guests over for lunch and I planned to make sandwiches. I glance at the clock and realize I need to go shopping now, in this window of time after the baby has eaten, but before he's due for his first nap—a quick trip to the store. Because the grocery store is less than a mile from my house and I only need a few items, I am optimistic. A quick trip to the store is entirely possible.

My first goal is to outfit the family in shoes and socks. I start with myself, because I'm the most cooperative. My baby Miles is next. I put on his socks and then his coat. He pulls off his right sock. While I am putting it on again, he pulls off the left sock. I stretch a knit hat on his head, replace the socks and, thankful for the snaps on his coat, leave him sitting in the hall. Now I can devote my full attention to convincing my preschooler that it's time to go now. There will be plenty of time to color and play trains when we get back from the store, which if we could just go already, will be before he knows it. Persuading Eli to get dressed becomes easier when I agree that he can bring two coloring books in the car, even though we're driving eight-tenths of a mile: one coloring book for each minute. No problem. Once he is dressed and wearing shoes, I return to the hall to find the baby eating one sock and the other lying on the floor next to his hat. I expected that we'd be at the checkout by now, but we're just leaving the house.

Once we get to the grocery store I push the unwieldy cart with the truck on the front so Eli can steer his way through the aisles. I find the things I need with minor detours, including a white plastic car my son feels sure would be the perfect gift for my husband's birthday and the bag of chocolate chips (not on the list) that he manages to get into the cart. The baby yawns, and I know we've reached a critical stage. If we get home too late, he won't go down for his morning nap and the effects of a too-tired baby will domino through our day. I wheel my truck-cart to a relatively short checkout line. When Eli darts to the DVDs on the shelves just beyond the counter, I assume a classic maternal stance. With one hand on the shopping cart, I am ready to move forward, as though the slightest movement away from my destination would represent surrender. I look back to him, one arm outstretched, fingers reaching to take his hand, willing him to me as though my arm has magnetic power. "Not today," I say. "Come with me." After a thoughtful pause, he walks toward me. I hold his hand across the parking lot, unload the cart, buckle the baby in his car seat, walk around the car to let Eli in, wait for him to climb in his car seat so I can buckle him and then close the door. I take a deep breath as I walk around the car to the driver's seat, marveling that I could have forgotten that there really is no such thing as a quick trip to the store.

The trip was not the simple outing I had planned, and neither is motherhood. I have always wanted to raise children, but generally imagined them ages seven and older. I pictured doing schoolwork together and making cookies as they listened carefully to instructions and embraced learning. They would reason and be wonderful artists. These wise little friends would enhance my life, but not change it that much.

In reality, my family began with a newborn, tiny and helpless. His inherent sweetness was countered by his mysterious cries and unpredictable sleeping schedules. He was more interested in grabbing my hair than making cookies. And he did not reason.

Still, my baby amazed me. His big newborn eyes gazed at me with depth and understanding. I marveled at those adorable fingers balled in a fist and the graceful curve of his ears. I loved this baby more than I could have imagined. When I sang to him, I could barely finish, "I Am a Child of God" without weeping. I knew he had been sent from his loving Heavenly Father to my earthly home. Humbled and awed, I felt over and over the miracle of this gift, God's own wonderful spirit in a tiny little body. Over time, though, and sleepless nights and countless dirty diapers, that sense of wonder faded. The role of motherhood became routine. There is little to marvel over when pureed peas are splattered across the kitchen floor, or I'm up with the baby for the third time in one night. At times, the beautiful moments seem lost, and motherhood looks like exhausting, thankless work.

When my list of things to do is especially long, I feel like I'm putting together a jigsaw puzzle. I choose an activity that fits the shape of the time I have. Because I can't do certain things while my baby is awake, I save them for his naptime. If folding laundry is next on my list, but he's asleep, I'll put that aside for later. I can play peek-a-boo while I fold the towels, but I can't answer emails with him on my lap. This thinking cycles throughout my day. Grocery store: now, before the baby's nap. Writing: later, when the boys are in bed. Weeding: now, when we can all go outside. Shuffling these puzzle-piece tasks is an important part of caring for my family and our home. I keep all the pieces on the table, choosing which to place where and when, always hoping they'll make the picture I see in my head.

But I woke up one morning this week thinking of the philosopher in Kensington Gardens. A gift of memory, I remembered the tragedy of naming a beautiful thing and then dismissing it. Arranging and rearranging, trying to find the puzzle pieces that best match my expectations, I have missed an essential element of appreciating each moment, no matter how it measures up to my ideal. I have rearranged that sense of acceptance so often that I have almost lost it. In the name of diaper changing and sleepless nights, what was I not seeing?

And then I knew. Focusing on what I thought motherhood should look like, and then feeling disappointed when it didn't measure up, I was missing the beautiful reality of my life with kids. My first gift from my little boy was a small rock from our yard that he dropped into my hand with chubby little fingers, gesturing that it was for me. When he's feeding sometimes, my baby will stop swallowing and look up at me and giggle, then go back to his lunch. At age two-and-a-half my oldest son wrapped his arms tightly around my neck and said, "Oh, Mommy, you're so cute." These are small details of ordinary or even exasperating days. Yet in these simple events, I feel true joy, sure of God's love for me and the tiny people I care for. To miss these beautiful moments because I'm looking for something else would be like calling it motherhood, and walking by.

The Hand of the Lord

by Lindsay Hepworth

I couldn't move my hand.

It was a scary realization to come to after just waking up from surgery. A month before, I had had the same surgery on my other shoulder and I didn't have any problems.

I waited for a few minutes to see if it was just asleep. It wasn't. The doctor confirmed that he had to stretch a nerve during surgery and that my hand would be temporarily paralyzed as a result.

As the weeks went by and I lived life with one working hand, I began to realize that you never know how much you use your left hand until you lose it.

I couldn't hold dishes as I washed them. I couldn't curl my hair. The sign language class I registered for at BYU that fall wasn't going to be easy. Typing was much slower when I had to hunt and peck. And, as I realized in the bathroom on my first day at BYU, zipping and buttoning cropped khaki pants that opened on the side was impossible. (I'll be forever grateful for the kind girl that helped me in the bathroom that day.)

But, despite the impossibilities, I got used to primarily using my right hand. I only had the option to use my right, so I did, and my right hand got stronger.

Although it was commonplace for me to do everything with my right hand, when I told people my left hand was paralyzed, they were amazed at the things I could do. They wanted to know how I was majoring in journalism without being able to type. They wanted to know how I could still play the piano. They wanted to know how I could do so much with just one hand. And secretly, I think they wondered if I would ever be able to do the things I used to do.

I wondered, too.

But, when I wondered I worked harder. I exercised. I worked on my physical therapy and my concerns began to fade. I gained some strength back in my left hand and I began compensating with my right for the things my left hand couldn't do.

And, eventually, with a little twitch there and another little twitch here, my left hand started to move again.

When I got divorced and became a single mother, the shock of the responsibility and independence that were suddenly on my shoulders was a lot like the shock of realizing my left hand was paralyzed. I would no longer have a partner to help me during middle-of-the-night episodes. I would have to live on my income. I could no longer be a stay-at-home mom. I would have to figure out a way for me and my 20-month-old little boy to make it on our own.

But, just like my right hand compensated for my left, I compensated for my lost partner. I found a job. I got insurance. I found support. And, I even had someone to help me do the things I couldn't possibly do my own. (I'll be eternally grateful for my parents and family that helped me during those days.)

I got stronger and soon it didn't even faze me that I was a single mother.

Although it was commonplace for me, my friends were amazed at what I could do. They couldn't understand how I could make it through the day without having relief when Daddy came home. They didn't know how I could discipline Garrett without the threat of "when your father gets home." And, although they never voiced it, I'm sure they were concerned that Garrett might never learn how to throw and catch a ball and play superheroes and villains with his action figures.

And, although I looked strong to them, inside I had those same concerns.

I was concerned when I took Garrett to his first day of all-day preschool and left him there to cry as I left on my way to work. His teacher assured me that he would be OK, but as I climbed the stairs out of his basement classroom, my little baby's cries echoed in my ears and I started to cry, too.

I got in my car and turned off the radio and did what I always did when I was faced with those concerns: I wiped my tears and began pleading with my Heavenly Father to help me make it through. I begged him to watch over my little boy. I asked him to help Garrett make friends. I asked him to help Garrett to remember to tell his teacher when he needed to go potty. I asked him to hold my baby when I couldn't and to dry his tears when I couldn't kiss them away. After pleading during my whole twenty-minute commute, I left my little Garrett in the hands of his Creator, wiped my tears, stood up straight, and I went to work.

I made it through midnight wakings and potty training and playgroups and time-out chairs with a constant prayer in my heart and consistent faith that although Garrett's earthly father couldn't help me, his Heavenly Father could. And when Heavenly Father's comfort wasn't enough, he sent me angels to help.

When I was playing Teenage Mutant Ninja Turtles with two-and-a-half-year-old Garrett, Heavenly Father sent my brother in to teach me how to play action figures like boys do.

When I needed to go out, Heavenly Father helped me by sending my mom or a cousin or one of my sisters to baby-sit.

When I needed to know I wasn't insane for feeling like being a mother was hard, Heavenly Father sent me friends to talk to and learn from every month at book group.

As I put more and more of my life in my Heavenly Father's hands, my Heavenly Father made me stronger and helped me to compensate for a missing earthly father. And, when he knew the time was right, he sent me in the path to meet a new companion.

As I relax on the couch with my wonderful new husband, I feel whole again. He turns off the TV and announces that it's time for bed. He takes a final walk around our apartment turning off lights, and he pauses to check on Garrett and make sure he's not turned around in his bed. He's made that his special nightly chore.

I stay on the couch waiting for his report about how Garrett's feet were on the pillow and I realize that my friends were right to be amazed that I ever did this on my own. We kneel to pray and my husband takes my still slightly lame left hand in his. And, although I no longer plead for the Lord to help and support Garrett and me, I pray for strength to help our new little family grow and become strong just like my left hand finally regained its strength. And, I know with a little twitch there and another little twitch here, He will help.

Towers

by Elaine B. Vickers

My son Jack and I have a game that we like to play together. It's pretty simple. I build a tower with his alphabet blocks, and then he knocks it over. I have read many times that toddlers love routines; for this game, we have certainly developed one. I sit on the floor in the family room, wearing sweats, my hair pulled back and probably unwashed. (This is often the state of my personal hygiene until ridiculously late in the day.)

I build a square base of four blocks, then put a single stack of blocks on top, adding as many as possible before the inevitable demolition. Jack plays with other toys as I perform this task, then runs over with his wobbly, one-year-old stride and knocks the tower over with whatever part of his body meets the top of my creation. If it's a short tower, he'll stick out his round belly to push it over. If he has granted me the time to build a taller tower, he'll bend at the waist and tip it over with his forehead. Then he smiles and gives a little chuckle and resumes playing with his trucks, and the process begins again. Four blocks for the base, a stack of blocks on top, and then the tower comes down again. We play this game several times each day.

My life was not always this way. Just two years ago, I was finishing up a Ph.D. in chemistry at the University of Utah. I had a husband and church responsibilities and friends, but my life was largely focused on academics and research. I was very goal-oriented, and my life proceeded in a fairly linear manner toward that goal. I wanted a Ph.D. There was a handbook given to each new graduate student outlining the steps required to earn this degree, and I had completed almost all of them. There were setbacks, sure, but mostly there was progression. We would sometimes joke in the lab that we were going to pee in each other's reactions, but we never actually did. (At least not to my knowledge.) We helped each other move forward, and when one reaction or project was completed, we moved on to the next one.

And so it came to pass that, eight months pregnant and knowing that I was near the end of my graduate school journey, I waddled to the front of the room to defend my thesis in front of a committee of stern-looking professors who were some of the leading researchers in their field. I bought a nice new maternity shirt. I went over my presentation again and again. Everything was prepared, and I knew that it would be a success.

And I passed. It wasn't perfect, but they signed my papers and shook my hand and said they were proud. My fellow graduate students had a party for me where they drank champagne and I drank root beer and they toasted my success. And I will forever have a piece of paper in a fancy frame that pronounces me Elaine Vickers, Ph.D.

Fast forward two years to the present. I'm now expecting my second child, a little sister for Jack whom we've decided to name Halle. I put my hard-earned degree to use by teaching part-time at the local university and earning disgracefully small paychecks. I still have my husband, my church responsibilities, and my friends, but now my life is focused on playing all the different roles of mother for one little boy and preparing to welcome his baby sister.

Some days, I'm just trying to keep my head above water. I'm just trying to maintain my sanity and keep Jack from seriously injuring himself and find time to clean the toilets before they develop a telltale smell. But some days, I feel that I can go above and beyond. I feel that I can be a great mom, and I am. I build a little tower of accomplishments. These are the days when I organize play dates and write in Jack's journal and go to story time at the library (against Jack's will) and exercise while Jack is napping and clean the toilets even though the telltale smell is weeks away. Today was one such day. Until bath time, that is, when the tower came tumbling down around me.

I received an email from a friend telling me that he and his son, who is just about Jack's age, love to go "swimming" together in the bathtub. I thought this was a fantastic idea and determined that I would try it out that very night. Jack usually likes bath time anyway, and I was in Supermom mode, after all. I decided Jack's tub was too small and filled my big, jetted tub with water that was just the right temperature. I got all of the best bath toys. I managed to encase my third-trimester body into a non-maternity swimsuit. In my most convincing, excited voice, I told Jack that we were going to go swimming together! My husband Robbie asked me if I needed any help, and I waved him away and told him he could go make his phone calls for Scouts the next day. Robbie was skeptical, but I was Supermom. Everything was prepared, and I knew that it would be a success.

Chemical reactions in the lab can be unpredictable, but motherhood is something else entirely. My new experiment set off a reaction that I never would have predicted and still don't comprehend. Jack started crying the moment that he set foot in the tub. Not just a little whimper, but a wail. His whole body went stiff and his face turned red. Little wet trails streamed from his eyes and nose. Then he started stomping and gasping for breath and trying to climb out of the tub. And since he was filthy and needed a bath, I couldn't just let him out. I still had to wash his whole body. Meanwhile, I tried everything I could to save the day, including a variety of songs and animal sounds and dumping water on my own head. But the crying only got worse.

By the time I had finished washing Jack, a bewildered Robbie came through the door to find us both in tears. "What happened?" he asked.

I managed to get out short sentences between my own somewhat irrational, pregnancy-induced sobs. "I don't know. I was so sure he'd love it. . . . Please, take him."

"OK, OK—it's OK. But why are *you* crying?"

"I failed again . . . and he hurt my feelings."

Robbie took Jack and calmed him down and put on his pajamas while I heaved my awkward body out of the tub and dried myself off. By the time I was in my own pajamas and ready to try again, Jack was already asleep.

Two years ago I was in a high-tech chemical lab synthesizing new molecule-based magnets. Now I am having disastrous "swimming" incidents and building block towers. As I sulk, I think of all the towers I've built that day—the dishes I've washed that will soon be dirty again, the beds I've made that will soon be unmade, the clean diaper that will all too soon be dirtied. All of my work undone, again and again, with few variations. And what is the reward? Jack doesn't shriek with laughter every time the block tower comes down. He doesn't throw his arms around my neck and thank me for building it each time. And he sure didn't like my bath idea.

As a mother, I wasn't given a handbook telling me the steps that I needed to take to be successful. All day, I'm in the company of someone whose sole purpose sometimes seems to be to undo what I've done, to sometimes quite literally pee in my reaction. At the end of the day, there's no group of colleagues to toast my success. There will never be a moment when a committee of well-dressed professionals shakes my hand and tells me that I'm finished, that I passed, never mind a piece of paper with my name on it to put in a fancy frame. But I'm grateful that there's no diploma for motherhood. It's not a task to be completed, not a set of hoops to jump through. I'm grateful not just because it's eternal, but because it's far too important.

The parenting books will tell you that kids sleep a lot because their bodies are growing. I think that's only part of the reason. I think God planned it that way so that we could watch our kids sleeping. Because tonight I walked into Jack's room and felt the gentle rise and fall of his chest and saw his fingers curled around the worn edge of his blanket and found everything I needed to wake up and build the towers all over again.

The Right Fit

by Josie L. Lee

Had I been interviewed for a position as a Mormon mother before my son was born, I might have made it through a couple of rounds. But in the end, despite my book-filled hours of preparation, my application would have been rejected because of "motivational fit"—a term I used frequently in one of my pre-parenthood jobs. As part of this job, I conducted behavior-based interviews with candidates looking for employment with our company. I would ask these candidates a series of questions designed to gauge their experience and proficiency across a range of competencies related to the open position (for example, teamwork, leadership, ability to multi-task and handle stress). Interestingly, candidates could score highly across the target areas and still not be hired because they were not the right "motivational fit." In other words, their personalities and aspirations were not cut out for the job, regardless of their skill sets.

Since, for a variety of reasons, I was not cut out for a position in Mormon Motherdom (or so I thought) I contemplated parenthood somewhat reluctantly. When Noah was born, however, I was overwhelmed by how much I unexpectedly adored him, and I entered motherhood like a lovesick bull in a china shop. No finesse. No technique. Just freehand gung ho.

I happily, if clumsily, assumed the necessary tasks and roles of motherhood, hoping the animal-instinct love in my gut would cover for my lack of fit. I didn't know what I was doing, but even heaven could not help anyone who messed with my boy.

As time passed, I began to feel more at ease in my new role. Somewhere in the hours of gazing at my baby and kissing his toes, the issue of motivational fit became irrelevant. Still, I was not fully comfortable in my new role as a Mormon mom, and there were moments when my inner china shop bull reared her ugly head. Unfortunately, at least one of these moments occurred in public.

It was a (dare I re-live this in print?) family home evening exchange—an ingenious invention unofficially introduced into the Church no doubt by an achieving mother of eight with a perfect motivational fit score. As the idea goes, a group of ten parents get together and exchange family home evening lessons they have prepared and copied for each member of the group. At the end of the exchange, all the parents walk away with instructions and materials for ten lessons to share with their families. In our stake, these exchanges had been going on for some time among the women, but I had never participated. I had no artistic skills or child development expertise to offer the group, and though I really liked the idea in theory, it required a little too much organization and attention to detail for my taste. Since family home evening in my childhood home never involved plans or visual aids, preparing a reproducible lesson didn't feel like something I was cut out for. This time, however, a dear friend of mine, whose mothering I greatly admired, persuaded me to participate in the exchange. She assured me that whatever I produced would be acceptable for the group. Forgetting my friend was not aware of the depth of my incompetence, I foolishly believed her and signed up.

This particular exchange was headed up by a young mother in our ward with a formidable motivational fit profile. During the months preceding the actual exchange, she organized several groups of ten mothers, no member of which would repeat a lesson topic. She compiled email lists, organized spreadsheets and kept us all informed of our collective progress with commanding precision.

I was impressed with her logistical management, but I was confused as to why people needed so much time and information to prepare. My all-heart, no-skill approach to parenting only required a few minutes to cobble together a family home evening lesson while clearing Monday's dinner dishes. Still, I took the cues from our fearless leader ("Only a month left until the exchange, Ladies!") and decided to ramp up.

The day before the exchange I sat down at the computer and typed two scriptures and a few simple activities related to gratitude: write a letter thanking a family member for something, make a list of things you're grateful for, say a prayer of gratitude. Going the extra mile, I found a black and white picture online depicting something vaguely related to gratitude and included it in my packet for children to color. My topic was clearly the lowest hanging fruit available, but in my misguided mind, I had done my due diligence in preparing. I naively hummed a primary song as I stood over the Xerox machine watching it spit out ten copies of the most involved family home evening lesson I had ever planned.

That night, we met some ward members at the bowling alley to celebrate a friend's birthday. Over a slice of pizza, I struck up a conversation with one of my husband's colleagues. Seeing he was alone with his two children I asked,

"Where's your wife?"

"Oh, she was tired. She stayed home to sleep."

Assuming she was experiencing the normal mother-of-small-children fatigue I knew too well, I flashed an empathetic smile. "Yeah, she pulled an all-nighter last night," he continued.

Since we were in a graduate student ward at the time, I assumed she had been up late studying. "Oh, really?" I replied, "I didn't know she was a student."

"She's not," he corrected me. "She was awake all night making family home evening packets for the exchange tomorrow."

My stomach churned. I tried not to look surprised as my mind began to review all the possible scenarios that would keep someone up all night preparing a lesson. A sticky key on the computer? Trouble with the copy machine? A heavenly visitation? The outer limits of my imagination could not comprehend what would have taken so long. Confused and uneasy, the rest of our conversation was a blur. I only know that I walked away from the party with the understanding that this woman had hand water-colored each of the ten lessons she prepared.

The next morning, the phrase "all-nighter" still ringing in my ears, I watched the women file in the student housing center for the exchange. At least half of them were perfect strangers to me, and the other half I knew only superficially. Among them was the remarkable spreadsheet wizard who managed the whole event. Her ever-competent presence made me nervous.

As I shuffled my packets and made small talk, I reminded myself that the woman who had been up all night is an artist—an anomaly. Surely water-coloring is not the norm. We gathered in a circle so each mother could explain her lesson.

I wish I could relate the play-by-play of the subsequent 30 minutes, but in the name of emotional self-preservation, I have long since repressed the details. All I remember is that as we began, each mother, in show-and-tell format, passed out a premium quality, intricately constructed masterpiece. As the first few lessons were explained, I consoled myself. *These were the overachievers. Every group has to have a few, right?* But as more lessons emerged from packets, it became painfully apparent that everyone in the room had been operating under a different set of criteria than I had been. No one had produced anything even remotely resembling the shoddy, black and white embarrassment I held in my sweating hand. By the time number eight and nine took their turns, the whole thing was a haze. There were three-dimensional figures, board games, diagrams with removable parts, illustrated stories, puzzles, inflatable visuals, line-by-line instructions, songs, recipes, age-appropriate adaptations, and on and on. I was astounded. My mind raced to find an urgent reason to leave the room with my packets in tow. But my usual gift for making excuses failed me. There was no way out.

OK. I'll just apologize sincerely for the quality of my lesson and move on. So this is not my Magnum Opus. Who cares? Resolved, I stood up. As I began handing out my packets, however—the very last to volunteer—I suddenly started to cry. *Stop. You've got to be kidding. It's Saturday morning in the Hasbrouck Community Center—we're not curing cancer here. Your packet is humiliating enough. Just breathe.* Despite my best efforts, I couldn't stop the tears. I sobbed uncontrollably as I explained the world's most substandard lesson on gratitude.

The lovely members of my group did their best to reassure me with sympathetic comments about the beauty of simplicity. But I knew that I was nothing short of the clever virgin whose idea it was to bring a half-ration of oil (only there weren't four others to help me explain myself or keep me company in the cold). What's worse—and what must have brought on the tears—was the unmistakable, public revelation that I was indeed the wrong motivational fit for Mormon motherhood. I was clearly disinclined to do things my peers did—even my good faith attempt was a complete failure. Though I knew that successful mothering could take on many forms, in that moment, I felt like a hack. I needed to see Noah to remind me that no one could love him more or better than I could—that despite my poor showing that morning, I was the perfect fit for him. But he was at home with Dad.

Several weeks later, the ten bulging packets I took from the exchange sat on the sofa. My recently-baptized friend had come to visit and, new to family home evening, she anxiously perused the lessons. Thankfully, she didn't know about my debacle. So, still stinging from post-traumatic exchange stress, I happily handed the packets over to her. *Have at it, Sister. Happy FHE to you.* Now a year and a half later, I'm more comfortable in my rhythm as a mother—be it as it may. And I really want my hard-won lesson packets back. Noah is almost three, and he would love to spin the three-dimensional wheel depicting baptism by immersion.

Tonight, however, I rest my pregnant belly on my thighs and watch Brandon, my always-adept husband, teach a home evening lesson he imagined on his way home from work. He opens the Bible to John chapter 10 and reads, "I am the good shepherd, and know my sheep, and am known of mine...and I lay down my life for the sheep." He quietly explains to Noah that a shepherd is someone who takes care of sheep, who feeds them and finds them when they are lost. Jesus, he tells him, is called the good shepherd because he cares for us. Brandon takes Noah by the hand and walks him to the computer to show him a picture of Christ surrounded by sheep. Pointing to Jesus' staff, Brandon leaves the room and returns with a hook-shaped umbrella. He hands it to Noah and proceeds to remove the white pillows from the couch. These, he explains as he places them gently on the floor, are our sheep and we are the shepherds. Following his dad's lead, Noah walks with staff in hand through the pillows, pausing to tenderly stroke each one. Brandon takes a small houseplant from the shelf and hands it to Noah. Together, they crouch to feed the sheep grass from the terracotta pot. No packets tonight. No motivational fit. Just the doctrines of the kingdom distilling like dew on my little family. Before long, Noah has pulled all the pillows from the couch—red and green and orange—and is dancing among the sheep.

Labor and Delivery

by Jenny K. Call

Labor

"UGH! . . . Flush.

I'd rather be throwing up my breakfast at home in my own toilet instead of the staff bathroom at the hospital. I can hear the call lights going off, but I need a minute to regroup. After a quick look in the mirror to check for vomit on my scrub top, I can run back to take care of my labor patients and the rest of the floor. Could I really have nearly eight more months to go before I end up back here as the patient instead of the nurse?

In Room 160, Super Mom is talking on her cell phone.

"Steve, after your AP Biology review, make sure you pick up the twins from soccer and don't forget to pick up your tuxedo for the dance. Oh, and could you pull the whites out of the laundry? Now put your sister on."

"Michelle, I need your help for a few days. Call Aunt Sally and ask her to call the family and tell them all that I am going to deliver the baby today. Make sure that Tim, Eric, Susan, Charlie, Steven, Richey, Melissa, and Eddie put their laundry in the bin. Make some dinner tonight—I think that I have some enchiladas in the freezer that you can warm up. Oh, and, tell your dad to come down to the hospital now because I am going to have this baby any minute."

I come into the room and ask how her how she is doing. She says that she is doing as well as can be expected, but since this is her tenth child, nothing can surprise her at this point. I take a second to check her and can't believe that she is almost eight centimeters dilated. Her oldest daughter, Mary, has come to help with labor. Mary is obviously pregnant and so I say, "Wow, this must be exciting to see your mom having her baby while you are pregnant with your first!"

"Oh, it's not my first." Mmmm. Open mouth and insert foot.

Mary proceeds to pull out her cell phone and dial. "Honey, I am going to be here with Mom through the night, so you'll have to go over and have dinner with the kids. Take Bobby and Johnny with you—the diversion will be good for them." With that, she hangs up the phone and returns her focus to her mother's labor. "Mom, what can I do to help you?"

"Talk to your father about a vasectomy?"

Silence. "Well . . . ah . . . I'll check on you in a few minutes. If you need me, I am going down the hall to check on my other patients." It won't be long now, so I'll be back soon, but hopefully not soon enough to hear more about vasectomies.

In Room 158, European Mom is in early labor.

You see a lot of interesting things in labor but I have never seen this before: European Mom and presumably European Dad are in the throes of passion. They must do things differently in Europe. I've never been in a room where I had to check to make sure I was not in a bedroom but actually in a hospital room.

"How are you coping right now? Do you have a specific plan for labor?" I fall back on my standard list of questions, too uncomfortable to think of anything else.

"Oh, vee are zuper comfortable, vee believe labor to be—

how do you say in English? *Passionate!*" European Mom says.

"O . . . K." Not sure of what else to do, I shuffle down the hall to peek in on the other patients in labor

Down in room 156, Athlete Mom is laboring. I hear cheers. I feel like I've gone from the honeymoon suite to the sports bar.

The expectant father and several men—including the phlebotomy tech they recruited—hover near the television watching the NBA playoffs. They are giving each other fives and talking in loud voices. "Tim Duncan is unstoppable. Did you see that pick? . . . Man, I'm glad this place has cable!"

"Ooooow, these contractions are sure getting stronger!" she moans, seemingly to herself.

"Honeyyou'redoingsogreatjustkeepupthegoodwork," a less-than-enthusiastic voice offers from near the TV. His eyes never waver from the screen, and the words rush out before the ball is passed.

I've heard of dads being called the coach, but this is ridiculous. Obviously, Athlete Dad is not focused on the big game. I rush over to check her.

"How are you doing? Do you need anything?"

"I'm guess I'm fine. . . . I'm not sure that my husband realizes that this birth is not a sporting event and cheering 'Keep it up!' is not going to help me."

I go and break up the men. They grumble away from the TV.

Expectations are a funny thing in labor and delivery. It doesn't matter how many children you have or how many books you have read; you cannot predict or expect things to turn out how you thought they would. Labor is a journey. The destination is known to some degree, but the journey to this destination is filled with the unexpected. As another wave of morning sickness begins, I wonder what journey each of these moms will experience today and whether I will ever actually make it to *my* destination.

Arches National Park, Southeastern Utah, three and a half years later

My husband and I made a choice early on in Elsie's life that we would always bring her along and show her our exploring ways. We even took Elsie to Europe for three weeks at age two. She surprised us by acquiring an insatiable taste for Orangina, Kinder chocolates, and crepes.

One of our favorite activities is hiking, so we had planned a few days for relaxing and getting out in the wilderness. We also wanted to see one of Utah's iconic sites: Delicate Arch.

"Elsie, we are going to see Delicate Arch," my husband told our daughter. "Are you excited?" Every time, she would answer, "I love 'devil arch,' let's go there."

Our pilgrimage to Utah's unofficial symbol of red rock beauty began at the Arches National Park bookstore. My husband has this crazy plan to visit all the National Parks and Major League baseball diamonds while our kids are young. In order to commemorate our journeys, we bought Elsie a National Park Passport. Each National Park has a stamp and a sticker that you can use to remember your trip. We were excited to collect them all. We showed Elsie the National Park passport, the picture, and the stamp of Delicate Arch. For 12 dollars we had bought a lifelong memory.

As we drove along the road to the trailhead in our air-conditioned car, Elsie kept saying, "We go on hike. We go see 'devil arch'!" in her adorable two-year-old voice.

"Yes, Elsie, we are going to hike to Delicate Arch."

From the back seat: "Riiiiip." Clearly the Delicate Arch page of the passport is Elsie's favorite. I cringe and actually think I might go buy a new one. Oh well, maybe we can glue it back together.

The sun beats down on the three of us—104 degrees. A long climb up pink and orange slickrock to the top and around a pair of sandstone fins and we will reach our destination. The slickrock provides no respite from the scorching sun. Elsie is literally huddled down under her sun hat in her backpack, her nose crinkled up and her lips pressed together in her trademark face of disapproval. We are all sweating like crazy. From within the backpack cavity, we hear:

"I hate this hike. I hate this 'pack pack.'"

"Ba-Ba, we only have to go up this hill," my husband tells her.

"I hate this hike. I hate this pack pack."

"I hate this hill. I hate this backpack, too," I hear my husband mutter under his breath.

I look up at the hill my husband just talked about and I can barely see the top. I hate this hike. I hate this hike.

"Elsie, let's sing a song," I offer to amuse us all amidst the drudgery of this slickrock wasteland.

"Pearly shells, pearly shells, from the ocean . . . " I start into a family favorite that has saved us many a time.

"No, not that song," Elsie whines. When "Pearly Shells" doesn't work, we know we are in trouble. I try six or seven other songs to redirect Elsie.

Finally, Elsie says, "No singing."

We hike further up the hill in total silence. Near the top of the hill, the wind begins to blow.

"Wind . . . no swiping," I hear Elsie say. We have got to stop watching so much *Dora the Explorer*, I think to myself.

We finally crest the hill. I am now carrying the backpack. Elsie likes to trade between Mom and Dad and we appease her like we always do. In good fun, her sometimes dictatorial ways have earned her the nickname of "Fidela Castro." We march forward, looking for lizards and trying to ignore the sweat running down our backs.

The last part of the trail has been blasted out from the side of a hulking sandstone dune that reaches way up into the sky above our heads. This dune masks any view of the arch until the final moment you see it. . . . Delicate Arch. We did it!

"Devil arch, devil arch!" Elise calls out excitedly. "Let's go under it."

AHHH. What a relief to unload that backpack and take in the breathtaking scenery. We all agree that this is way better than the ripped picture of Delicate Arch falling out of the passport. There are few places in the world that when you finally reach them they leave you awestruck. Delicate Arch defies our expectations.

Delivery

"Ten centimeters," my nurse says to me with relief and excitement.

"You can do this, we are almost there," my husband says as he leans in to give me a kiss on the check.

Days of latent labor and multiple medical interventions that I didn't anticipate and we are finally here. This is what it feels like to see the light at the end of a tunnel.

"PUSH."

We settle into a rhythm. I push, the nurse counts, and my husband holds my hand and gives me ice in between contractions. An hour goes by, then another. I'm almost there. I can do this.

"Just a couple more pushes, nice and easy."

"PUSH!"

There she comes.

Silence.

"Is she breathing?" I ask in desperation.

Something is not right. My nurse-midwife rubs my little girl to stimulate her but no response. Around me, my hospital colleagues pick up my baby and rush to get the bag and mask together to give my child some life-saving breaths.

I can't breathe. I can't think. I am exhausted from days of awful labor.

The seconds pass and I am in shock. How can this be happening? Tears spill onto my cheek. I say a quick prayer. How many other prayers are being said in this tiny room?

"Heavenly Father, please let my baby breathe."

"Wa-wa." Elsie's first cry . . . the most beautiful sound, an answer to prayer. In seconds I am holding my creation. Elsie, my husband, and I united as a family on my hospital bed for a few precious moments. Soon, the doctors and nurses are telling me that they must rush Elsie to the nursery because she has had a difficult journey getting to this earth. I tell my shocked husband to go with the baby to the nursery.

Lying in my hospital bed, alone for the first time in days, physically numb from an epidural, I marvel at the miracle of birth—*my* baby's birth, not someone else's.

Clinically, I understand this process well. Experientially, I now see the hand of God.

Life's best journeys—whether they be delivering a baby or hiking to Delicate Arch—require tremendous effort. Sometimes you have to ignore the feelings of inadequacy or reluctance, such as "I hate this hike. . . . I hate this pack pack. . . . I hate this labor. . . . These kids are driving me nuts!" You have to keep going because the next bend in the road might reveal a vision of divinity.

Not all the laboring patients I have cared for in the hospital have been blessed with this vision. We each come into labor with different ideas and expectations. I'm sure Athlete Dad did not expect to miss the end of the game because of a c-section. I bet European Mom didn't expect to find labor so painful. We each take a different path to get to our destination. Sometimes a mother is completing the journey for someone else and will give her baby to another person and enable her to begin her journey of motherhood.

And sometimes there is no Delicate Arch. Sometimes the hot, sweaty hill keeps on going. Sometimes you are left with a heartache that only the Lord can mend. At times we say to ourselves "I hate this hike. I hate the load I am carrying." But we have to keep on trudging because with a loving Heavenly Father there are always more hills to climb and beautiful vistas and blessings to find and trudging along for now is all we can do.

Mothers are particularly blessed among God's children because they get a private glimpse of his divinity through labor and delivery and the continued blessing of motherhood. We must continue our journey; whether we are are traveling through a beautiful landscape dotted with red rock arches or a never-ending emotional desert of punishing slickrock. Heavenly Father is our Deliverer. I will always be grateful for my beautiful daughter—my Delicate Arch—and the journey I had to go through to get her.

Boarding the Straight and Narrow

by Connie Merrell Sowards

Tomorrow was the day. Tomorrow the big yellow bus that had stopped in front of our house day after day was going to be there to transport you to the best and most exciting place in the world—Kindergarten!

Your intangible excitement had been growing steadily ever since we went to the school together to register. You met your new teacher and you fell in love with her instantly. The walls of our home echoed with your oft-repeated descriptions of that cute kindergarten classroom. The level of excitement swelled until it became too big to be contained in only one person. Anticipation was bouncing off the walls. I couldn't help but feel butterflies in my stomach as I watched you carefully pick out what you would wear for that first day and lay it out neatly at the end of your bed. You were eager to start your normal bedtime routine, knowing from years of Christmas Eve experience that going to bed early would hasten the arrival of a much anticipated tomorrow.

Up to this point in your life I had been in control of almost every aspect of your existence, and my approval was all that you needed to be happy. As I sat alone on that warm August night,

I reflected on the many priceless hours we had spent together over the last five years: hours reading books at naptime, playing at the park, singing songs in the car, and so many more. It was almost too much for my heart to bear to think of sending you away to be at the mercy of others who didn't know you as intimately as I did, who wouldn't immediately recognize your needs, who couldn't read the looks on your face, and who would not be there to shield you from hurtful things others might say. And then there was the thought of recess. Who would you play with? What if someone was mean to you? Would you be brave enough to make new friends? Would you recognize right from wrong? Would you be able to leave the protective presence of your teacher?

There seemed to be a never-ending list of things for a mother to worry about. Added to that worry was the aching of what seemed to be the start of a small hole in my heart as you gained your independence and didn't need me as much. I started to realize that though I was fully grown, I was still subject to growing pains. It hurt me to realize that my little girl was growing up.

My worries soon fled. The first day of kindergarten was a huge success. You stepped off of the big bus steps proudly, your backpack squarely on your shoulders, and proceeded to walk down the sidewalk in a rather dignified manner. We didn't even have to ask how your day was because you started talking the moment we were within earshot and couldn't seem to stop talking about how wonderful it was and how great a time you had. You pulled each of the papers your teacher had sent home out of your backpack one at a time, and with such care, that your sister and I could really tell you felt like an official kindergartner.

Day two was different. The bus pulled up to drop you off and we watched the kids file down the stairs. We had missed you and were eager to see your cute kindergarten face again. The last kid stepped down, the door closed, and the brakes of the bus sighed loudly as they released. I was standing up, straining nervously to see if any children remained on the bus. Our house was the last stop and the bus looked empty. I raced to the bus and tried not to look panicked as I rapped on the door to get the bus driver's attention. The bus driver seemed familiar with these types of situations and calmly radioed in our predicament. You had ended up on another bus and would be dropped off after that bus made its entire run. We sat nervously on the porch and waited.

I don't think I will ever forget the terrified, yet relieved, look on your face as you flew down the giant steps of the bus and began to run to our front steps. Your backpack was bouncing wildly. I guess it hadn't made it over both shoulders in your frantic scramble to get off of that other bus. Uncertain of how to react, I just sat there on the steps with my arms open wide, anxious to see how you handled such a frightening experience. You flung yourself into my relieved embrace, and as you looked into my face you did your best to fight back your tears.

You admitted that you had cried a little bit on the bus. I told you it was OK to cry, and I just held you as your kindergarten pride got washed away in the flood of your relieved sobbing. "I was missing you so bad, Mom," you said over and over again. You told me how you thought you would never find your home, that you were afraid you would have to sleep on the bus, and that Dad and I would cry and miss you so much and not know where you were. Even after we went inside, we held each other tight. Your tears soaked my shoulder as my tears fell silently into your hair. I was so relieved to have you safe, but my heart ached for what you had been through. I had never seen my little girl so terrified.

It wasn't until much later that day, when the house was quiet once more, that I recognized that there was a lesson in these traumatic events. I thought, "How often do we mistakenly get on the wrong bus?" The comings and goings, the meetings and the rehearsals, the practices and projects can get us so sidetracked that we end up miles away before we know it. If we let the basic gospel guidelines take a back seat to modern modalities, our lives and spirituality will be far away from where they really need to be. Modern day revelation has told us that "successful . . . families are established and maintained on principles of faith, prayer, repentance, forgiveness, respect, love, compassion, work, and wholesome recreational activities," but how much of our day is filled with activities that help us develop these attributes? ("The Family: A Proclamation to the World," *Ensign*, November 1995, 102).

The real goal is to get ourselves and our families back to our Father in Heaven. We are an achievement-driven society. We want to be able to do it all, and we tend to want our children to have every possible chance for worldly greatness. But we need to be careful. Our attempts to fill our lives with "good things" can lead us to feel so proud and confident in our own abilities that we essentially "board the wrong bus." We may not realize until after the bus is moving that we are not in familiar places, nor are we surrounded by the people we love and cherish. It is our own desires and ambitions that have driven us away from the home and family we were sent here to nurture and nourish.

Elder Neal A. Maxwell said, "The home is usually the place where most of our faith is established and increased. How sad, therefore, that some homes are merely a pit stop, when they should be a prep school for the celestial kingdom" (*Lord, Increase Our Faith*, [Salt Lake City: Bookcraft Publications, 1994], 117).

It is my goal as your mother to make our home more of a prep school and not just a pit stop. I want it to be the right stop as you travel down the road of life. The Lord has given us guidelines to help us make our homes havens of spiritual learning and love. He has also outlined programs within the church to help strengthen us individually and to expand our home into a place where the Spirit can reside as we promote learning and love. Daily scripture study as a family can open discussions that help foster faith in Jesus Christ. Kneeling together as a family in daily prayer can build bonds that can strengthen us as we fight our daily battles. Weekly family home evenings can bring the family closer together and closer to the Lord through fun and games mixed with spiritual learning.

As we rush here and there during the unyielding minutes of each day, we can sometimes forget the important things that help us to stay headed in the right direction. Even I sometimes inadvertently "get on the wrong bus" and before long realize that the place I really want my family to be is miles away from our current position.

As your mother, I must always strive to put our family first and take advantage of the opportunities given us to develop and cultivate lasting family relationships. Working together, we must set aside the trivial and temporal and devote our lives to improving those things that are sacred and eternal.

There may come a day in your young life when you realize that you are seated comfortably on a bus that is moving in the wrong direction. I hope you always remember there is an open line of communication with one who sees your position no matter where the bus may take you. He knows the routes well and can help you find the quickest way back. He always knows how to turn things around. As you reroute your life and resolve to stay on the bus that is homeward bound, please remember that your loving and caring Heavenly Father is always available to help guide the way if you ask for his help. He will be watching and waiting with infinite wisdom to give you the comfort and encouragement you will need to keep going.

You can always begin anew with eagerness to move in the right direction. As you do so, Heavenly Father will ultimately give you the most personalized education you could ever ask for and daily direct your life for good. And when you arrive at your final destination, no matter how many wrong routes you may have taken, your Heavenly Father will be waiting, arms outstretched, with the boundless love a parent has for a child, and will welcome you home.

Everyday Pearls

by Jennifer E. Brown

It's almost 5:00 and I have to ask myself, what do I have to show for my day? I start chopping the carrots for dinner, hoping that the kids will stay happy for just a few minutes. So far so good. No one is crying—wait a minute, it's a little bit *too* quiet. Three-year-old Eric comes out of the bathroom with evidence of the excellent workings of his digestive system all over his hands. I keep it together with a barely suppressed sigh and run to see if he created a Monet or just a Picasso. Just as I finish damage control in the bathroom, baby Lily starts to yelp and I see that Eric has helped himself and the kitchen floor to some juice.

"Eric Timothy!"

That's it. I just invoked the power of the middle name and he knows that he has gone too far. I send him to timeout where he continues to whimper about juice. I resume my chopping, which has now become a vicarious punishment to the poor carrots. I try to salve my frustrated feelings by thinking of all the quotes I have heard about how motherhood is the most important, fulfilling job in the world.

Although I believe this to be true, I certainly don't feel important, or even competent, right now. The guilt is finding me. I overreact too often. I don't stimulate my children enough.

I don't do enough fun things. My house isn't spotless.

I go to open the fridge. Under a magnet I see a picture of my grandmother Melba. She is standing by their grand piano in an understatedly elegant white sheath dress with a long string of pearls around her neck. The soft lighting and the pastel colors of the room give her an almost ethereal glow. My grandmother was not a celebrity, but she always carried herself with the poise and grace of a true lady.

Although she died when I was only nine, I still remember the essence of my grandmother when I see pearls and yellow roses. She didn't even run errands (in her tennis shoes) without her string of everyday cultured pearls. She always seemed like a sweet, loving, elegant lady to me. I'm sure that *she* never remained un-showered until 2:00 p.m.

My grandmother raised five wonderful children, including a daughter with Down's Syndrome. As a child, I never remember hearing my grandmother raise her voice, even when my cousins and I probably deserved to be scolded. I later thought that perhaps I was seeing the finished product—that all of her life experiences taught her to be so patient. However, my father told me that he remembered her the same way, even as a young boy. She was constantly downplaying the significance of his mistakes. And he made some big ones: from stealing a handful of cheap pens from a stationery store, to launching sparklers across the basement, almost setting the house on fire. But to my grandmother, the *child* was always more important than the *thing*. And despite the inevitable setbacks, all of my grandmother's children turned into the kind of people I would like to become. I hope that maybe just a little bit of her character is genetic.

In fact, as I look at the pearls around Grandma Melba's neck, I realize that in many ways my grandmother was a genuine pearl. Pearls are formed when an irritant becomes trapped in an oyster's shell. The oyster coats the object with layers of a substance called nacre and after many years, the pearl is formed. My own wonderful mother said, "As I learned about Melba and her life, I learned that any fault she may have had as a young girl, she found to be an irritant and, over the years, she covered those faults with things such as education, kindness, generosity, courage, and love. Each thin layer added more to the luster of her character until, at the end of her life, I believe she was one of the most beautiful human gems."

As I think about the way my grandmother became such an exquisite pearl, I am reminded that the everyday irritants that I deal with inevitably lead to more memorable pearls: like when I am lying in bed with Eric and tickling his back before he goes to sleep. He sighs happily and says, "Mommy, I just love you so much!" Or when I gratify Lily's wish to be held and she lays her head on my shoulder and pats my back in approbation. Or when Eric plays peek-a-boo with Lily and makes her laugh hysterically. Or when I can nibble on their chubby parts. Or when I have the chance to dry their tears. There is nothing as soothing to a mother's guilt as being a comforter. As Henry Van Dyke said, "[a pearl] becomes more precious the longer it is carried close to the warmth of the beating heart."

Perhaps these moments wouldn't be as sweet without the daily irritants to give them contrast and added luster.

If nothing else, being a mother has increased my portion of love. I now understand the sacrifice of God's Only Begotten Son with a new heart. I have tasted a very small sample of the pain he must feel when we are hurting. I can understand how *desperately* he must want us to succeed.

And if I think about it, I'm really not such a bad mother. I am really good at a few things. I can usually stay ahead of my dishes. I try to read to my children and snuggle with them as often as I can. I am neurotic about getting at least five servings of fruits and veggies into my children every day. I keep their teeth brushed. Perhaps that is what my children will remember when they think of me—not yellow roses and pearls, but carrots and toothpaste.

I go to Eric, who is now sitting quietly in the time-out chair. I talk to him about why he is there and we end our discussion with a hug. Dinner finally makes it on the table and my kids have now eaten their veggies for the day.

I think about my grandmother and her great capacity for love. Maybe some of it is genetic. After all, Melba and I are immortally strung together. And while I am waiting for time and experience to make my luster as rich and warm as hers, I can try to reflect her luminosity. The potential is there, if I can just focus on what really matters and try to mother with love and grace. I am feeling much better. Maybe I will go put on some pearls.

Sane Mothers, Take a Bow

by Melissa Baird Carpenter

All the world's a stage, And all the men and women [and children] merely players.
— Shakespeare, *As You Like It*, Act II, Scene VII

When I think of my role as a mother, I often see myself as the director of The Carpenter Family Melodrama Show. As the director, I have the right to determine the props and set designs. However, once my little actors take their places on the stage, I have found that they are partial to improvisation. When things go wrong, my only recourse is to "cut" the action and discourage repeat performances. The unpredictability of how a scene will play out seems to be one of the most frustrating parts of my job. Take for instance one of last year's episodes of The Carpenter Family Melodrama Show titled "Petco Purgatory."

I secured my daughter into the seat of a shopping cart and my son walked beside me as I guided the cart and our dog to the back of the pet store. Nervous canines and their faithful owners stood in a line that extended from one end of the store to the other. We were there to get low-cost vaccinations for our dog Archie. Some of the more anxious dogs peed or pooped on the floor, while others barked to release some of the tension. Before I knew it, four-year-old Gabriel was spitting saliva onto the floor. Apparently the smell of stinky, sweaty dogs makes him feel like vomiting.

Meanwhile, my then one-year-old daughter, Corinne, stuffed pretzels into her mouth to entertain the elderly couple who let us go ahead of them in line (and who earned my undying gratitude). She had a poopy diaper, but I wasn't about to lose my place in line by going somewhere to change it, nor did I care when she removed her tennis shoes and put a dirty sock in her mouth.

With perfect timing, Gabriel announced that he had to go to the bathroom the moment we reached the register. He started crying, so I scooped him up into the now-unoccupied front seat and pushed the cart toward the vet's table. Time for shots.

Archie was doing just fine, but then my daughter saw the needles in the vet's hands and she started screaming—probably due to unpleasant memories of the shots she had received a month earlier. Well, that put Archie over the top, and he tried to jump off of the table, snapping his head around and hitting the doctor's hand. The cap came off of the needle and released its contents into the air, showering two unhappy people behind us with dog vaccinations. The doctor assured the customers that there would be no adverse effects. In the meantime, I pulled my daughter out of the cart with one arm and held onto Archie with the other. The vet gave three quick shots, and we were done.

We made it to the car, got loaded up, and started the drive home. I couldn't believe how disastrous that one hour had been. As if it hadn't been enough, Archie started dry heaving, and Gabriel reminded me that he was hungry and still needed to go potty. I pushed Archie onto the back seat, which was covered with a blanket, and handed a sandwich to my son. The rest of the drive home was filled with silence. As we pulled into the driveway my son said to me, "Wow, Mom, we had a lot of fun, didn't we?" I couldn't believe my ears. I was just glad to be home.

I unloaded the children, the dog, and the diaper bag from our car. We immediately started our bedtime routine of putting on pajamas, brushing teeth, and saying prayers. And yes, I finally got to change my daughter's diaper.

As a director, one of my strategies has been to write down all of the good material I come across. Motherhood can be a magnificent muse. So, after I got my mini minstrels in bed and all was quiet, I went into my home-office and took a moment to think about our latest adventure. The kids fell asleep right away and the stillness of the house restored a sense of calm to my unnerved demeanor. In order to regain my sanity, I immediately began to write about the experience. I replayed the scenes in my mind, alternately frowning and chuckling as I stared at my computer screen.

By reenacting the story, I was able to enjoy my troupe's plight as an audience member would. While it was still fresh in my mind and fresh off the presses, I attached the anecdote to an e-mail to my family and friends. Somehow just writing about the pet store fiasco and sharing it with others provided me with the comic relief I needed. That hour in the pet store had left me feeling flustered, but by recording an account of what had happened, I felt like I had more control over my life. I quickly realized that although the sequence of events had not matched my overall plan, the anticipated outcome had still been the same. Well, almost. I'm not sure if I had anticipated raining down dog inoculations on the heads of complete strangers.

While writing has been a significant strategy for me in dealing with the hectic lives that modern-day moms must lead, an even more effective one has been my job as a part-time teacher. I teach composition at a local community college. One of the advantages of teaching adults is that I don't have to spend my time disciplining others. In addition, I am able to develop lesson plans with the expectation that I will have the cooperation of my students. My experience in the pet store stands in stark contrast with a typical night in the classroom.

While my cast of students varies from semester to semester, we manage to follow the script each time, only deviating when an unanticipated learning opportunity presents itself. There are of course occasional disturbances to the learning process, but they seem minimal in comparison with the types of disruptions I encounter as the mother of two preschoolers. My job has allowed me to maintain mental equilibrium. I can deal with the chaos at home because I spend a few hours away from home every week.

Teaching is my slice of sanity; it has kept me connected to the world of adults, a world in which order usually carries the day. Maintaining my involvement in the academic community has also allowed me to hold onto a significant aspect of my pre-mommy identity. This experience has helped me understand that while a woman cannot venture into motherhood expecting to come out of it unchanged, she can discover ways to wed the person she was beforehand with her evolving persona.

When my son was 18 months old I attended a free class for parents and their children at our local community center. I met several moms there and we enjoyed getting to know one another during the five-week class. At the end of the program, one of the mothers suggested we start a playgroup of our own. For the first two years we met on a weekly basis. Sometimes we would meet at a park, the library, or the mall; other times we would rotate playgroups at someone's house. At first, we moms were a group of directors getting together to share ideas. As our band of players enjoyed their recreation, we swapped advice about how to get our children to share toys, how to work around baby's nap schedule, and how to potty train a two-year-old. The more experienced moms with slightly older children were open and honest about their past struggles. The younger moms were always willing to listen.

Nearly four years have passed since we met and although the number of moms has dwindled to four faithful friends, the number of children involved in the playgroup has almost doubled due to our growing families. Now with conflicting preschool schedules and extra-curricular activities, the playgroup is only able to get together once a month. However, we have started a new tradition of Girls Night Out. Every three months one of us moms chooses a restaurant and we all meet up for a couple of hours. While we initially formed a group because we were going through similar stages in our careers as mothers, our relationships now exist within and without the theater of motherhood. The friendships I have developed through the playgroup were pivotal in my transition from an inexperienced, insecure mother to a busy, and somewhat competent one.

We all have interests and activities that we give up or put on hold when we become mothers. Our time has to be carefully managed and oftentimes our kids, not our day planners, dictate our schedules. However, I have learned we each need to find activities that make us happy and pencil them into our lives. There will be times when a hobby or goal may not fit into our mommy calendars; nevertheless, we can save them for a future act when the timing seems more appropriate. In addition, we can focus on how becoming a parent has given us opportunities to bond with other moms. Not only has this period in my life allowed me to meet and befriend other women, it has also been a time when my relationships with longtime friends have deepened through our shared experiences as mothers. Best of all, we can preserve our sanity and develop our sacred identities while helping our children develop their own. When the applause and praise for our children comes, as it inevitably will, we can stand beside them, knowing we have played our part well. When the cue comes, we will all take a bow.

The Lord's Design

by Melissa H. Carlos

The great thing about a memory is that it is so easily recalled by a glimpse of something familiar, a sound, a nostalgic smell, or even a word. Today for me it is a book about California and I close my eyes and remember the way my life used to be before I became a mother.

It is 5:45 a.m. (a time that I decide should not be seen by rational humans) and I am getting ready for work. I go to the train station and 45 minutes later the train rolls to our final stop. I am out of my seat and ready to start the day. I am wearing my favorite long pink coat and the rest of my attire has tags that read, "dry clean only." I'm off the train and walking the final mile to the office because the scenery is too beautiful not to enjoy.

I see a program blow past me from last night's baseball game and Pac Bell Park is now quiet. The ocean smells of salt, and waves are steadily lapping the side of the pier as gulls hover above in a search for breakfast. A few yards later I come upon the Bay Bridge and, since it's a clear day, I can see all the way to Oakland. Large pink flowers sit in window boxes above a tiny sidewalk café with red striped awnings. I walk past it and through the door wafts the smell of freshly baked bread. The street scene looks like a painting and as the minutes roll on the city is starting to come to life.

I arrive at my office, where I am a graphic designer for one of the largest retailers in the world. I landed here after BYU graduation and a thankfully short-lived stint as a small company designer. Designing and using the degree I had worked for five years to earn is just as fulfilling as I imaged it to be. I love going to meetings, presenting my designs, and then seeing my work in stores all over the country.

As a working girl, my life has order. I have people and computer alarms to remind me when to do things. I eat sushi neatly packaged in little rows and follow my Outlook calendar to a T. For the most part, I do what I want, when I want to do it. Beautiful things and city scenery constantly surround me. I worked long and hard to get to where I am and I truly feel that my time working here is part of Heavenly Father's plan for me. He knows that this is exactly what I need at this time in my life and how glad I am that he knows because I love what I do.

I have always loved the challenge of trying to create beautiful things. I enjoy taking many different elements and seeing how and why they fit together to make something new and beautiful. In my early childhood I fulfilled this need by constantly drawing and coloring. (I was spurred on by my mother who I distinctly remember telling me how good my giraffe drawings were.) Later on it was painting. By the time I got to college, the giraffes were far behind me and I had moved on to graphic design, and to the life to which this vivid memory belongs.

I am jolted from my daydream by a tiny, yet determined cry, and I walk down the hall to retrieve my daughter from her crib. I am not in California, walking in the salty sea air to a job I love. I am in New York with my young daughter, whom I love even more.

Even though I enjoyed my career, I knew that what I really always wanted to do was have children and be a good mother to them. I always felt that my ultimate design was not going to be displayed in a storefront, but in a family photo album. I dreamt of days in the sandbox, cereal necklaces, and coloring books. I wanted to be the one who encouraged children to draw giraffes. Most importantly, I knew that being a mother and raising righteous children was ultimately Heavenly Father's plan for me. I knew that when the time came, I was going to enjoy it immensely.

I worked as a designer for two years before going through a horrific first trimester, and a fairly easy pregnancy. Finally, I met my Magnum Opus in the delivery room at El Camino Hospital—this was the creation I had waited so long to see! My husband and I were overjoyed to begin our journey through parenthood and for two days in the hospital we just stared at our baby girl and marveled that she was actually ours.

After those two magical days, we brought her home only to discover that at times our beautiful baby had a talent for chaos. She would cry for no apparent reason while we tried everything to console her. She was constantly awake and was impossible to get to sleep. (I would have given anything at that point to have 5:45 a.m. be the only time I woke up.) Sometimes during the day she would sleep only an hour and my husband and I would stare at each other dumbfounded. We felt it was such a miracle to have a baby, but now we needed another miracle to know how to take care of her. Our first journey into parenthood was turning into more of a melee involving this tiny baby and two previously intelligent adults. It also involved tears. Lots of tears. My mother came to stay with us and I distinctly remember begging her not to go home and leave me alone with my own child.

My mind quickly began to fill with questions. What had

my motherhood experience become? What happened to all the "skills" I thought I had in quieting, consoling and raising children? And why couldn't I turn this chaos into order? If I previously had such strong feelings about becoming a mother, why was it so challenging now?

The basic answer to these questions is that motherhood is hard. Sometimes it's really hard. I learned that having a baby means within a split second you have gone from taking care of two adults to taking care of another life that is completely dependent on you. I was lucky if I got a shower. I had less desire to see the light of day and more desire to be in my own bed as soon as the baby was quiet. It is off with the dry-clean-only and on with the jeans and t-shirt (that will probably be dirty in 15 minutes anyway). I became relegated to consuming whatever was on the kitchen counter because it was the easiest thing to grab and eat with one hand. (I distinctly remember one early breakfast consisting entirely of lemon bars brought by the neighbors.)

I worked my tail off five years through college and three years of working in the "real world." But having my first baby was far harder than either of these. She has pushed me and stretched me emotionally and physically to a breaking point. After settling into motherhood, I have decided that one of the hardest things is that there's no store window display to be complimented, no positive employment review, and no one to say thank you once the work is done. When I was a working girl the results of my day were so tangible—you could literally hold them in your hand. Now as I mother I work twice as hard and I distinctly remember one fine day when the only fruit of my labor was my favorite skirt soaking in the sink. I can't believe I actually got pooped on. (I'm told this is a motherhood rite of passage, but it didn't make me feel any better.) Within an instant my daughter disbanded the beautiful order that was my life, and, despite the disorder, I wouldn't want it any other way.

As I look past the dirty dishes, I realize that my life is beautiful in an unexpected way. There was nothing like the beauty of seeing my little baby smile at me for the first time. When my daughter was six months old she learned how to give kisses. She could just hear the word *kiss* and immediately I would receive a big, wet, slobbery kiss. Now I get unsolicited kisses multiple times a day. She also just learned to growl like a bear, and bob like a fish. These are joys that I certainly never got at work and they remind me how glad I am that I'm a mother.

My daughter is now a year old and has started giving her dolls loves. As I watched her give those babies loves until their little eyes practically popped out, it occurred to me that she was following my own example of love. She gave those dolls loves like I gave her loves. Seeing this was one of those parental moments where the joy wells up inside you and comes out as tears in your eyes. I quickly learned that with all the trials, she has also brought me the most joy I've ever felt. Being able to give love and see someone else give it in return makes me realize that with all the dirty diapers, spilled food, crazy schedules, and tears, my daughter is still able to recognize that I love her.

I know now that I don't need praise for a project well done in order have tangible results of my work. I get to hold, quite literally, the fruits of my labors at the end of the day. As my daughter snuggles into my neck after I pick her up from her nap, I am reminded once again that there's no better reward that I could hope for than for her to love me and feel my love in return.

Much like my motherhood experience, every time I have designed something it has started out as a chaotic mess. Graphic design, or any type of design, is just little bits of information, perhaps colors or pictures that have to be combined in a new way in order for it to make sense and be successful. Getting a design "right" on the first try is about as common as a hole-in-one when you're golfing—it's something that has to be worked and reworked until everything balances out. Design is about making small strides until you've created something better.

I have gained a greater testimony of the words of Nephi in 2 Nephi 28:30: "For behold, thus saith the Lord God: I will give unto the children of men line upon line, precept upon precept, here a little and there a little."

When I step back and look at my life, I realize that these same ideas apply to motherhood and our Heavenly Father's plan for us. His design for me as a mother is something that also must be worked out a little at a time. No matter how much we would like it to be, it will never be perfect on the first try—and lucky for us, the Lord will never expect it to be. He guides our lives and gives us beautiful children, but we are the ones who are responsible to bring order and balance to everything. We are the ones who must combine all life's elements in a pleasing and successful way and as we do so he will help us along. He helps us because as we carry out his most important work, he also desires that we find joy and success. This is his design.

Enjoy These Years, Dear, They Go By So Quickly

by Laurie Brooks

Every Tuesday morning at some point during our breakfast routine I expect to hear from my husky-voiced four-year-old as the first audible rumblings emerge from somewhere in the neighborhood. "Mom! It's trash truck time!" he exclaims. I return his excited look with my jaw dropped and my eyes wide as if I am as surprised as he is about the truck's arrival. As we clamor quickly to the door, we abandon toys and breakfast dishes so we can salute the large green machine before it passes by. Clayton reaches the door first, quickly flings open the screen, and rushes out onto the dewy-wet lawn. I follow behind in my bare feet and pajamas just as the truck screeches to a halt in front of our house and begins to feed its hopper our assortment of trash. Clayton carefully examines the process, overseeing the accuracy and wonder of the technique as only a young boy can do. I too am impressed at how smoothly the driver uses the truck's metal arm to maneuver each bulging load without spilling remnants onto the street.

Usually the driver takes notice of our presence, perhaps surprised at our warm reception to a job not usually met with fanfare. Before the driver moves on, he puts out his hand to answer Clayton's vigorous arm flapping. As we finish waving, Clayton bounds down the driveway to chase the truck until I beckon him back. Sometimes when he returns he self-assuredly reports, "Mom, I want to be a trash truck driver when I grow up!" I grin about this dream occupation for my boy, knowing it will likely change as time goes on and that for now it is the cutest little dream in the world.

This Tuesday ritual has kept me smiling since it began years ago when Clayton was no more than a baby who was innately enamored by trucks. At times I have impatiently hopped up and down on the cold pavement in my bare feet wishing the truck would go by so I could escape back to our warm kitchen. However, after years of sharing trash truck time with Clayton, I realize that school days will soon replace this time of enjoying carefree breakfasts and the neighborhood trash pickup together.

It has only been since I've become a mom that I have become quite conscious of the passing of time. It all began with the nine anticipation-filled months of pregnancy. During those months I was keenly aware of each week, knowing and feeling a growing miracle, which would soon become part of my life forever.

As the arrival of my first baby drew near, I was a magnet for even more friendly advice than I had been as a bride. I eagerly absorbed the advice I was offered by friends, family, neighbors, and even the grocery clerks. I figured I could use all the well-meant advice to help me solve the new mysteries I would face-- like which diapers were the best buy and how to soothe a crying baby to sleep. As the women at my baby shower took turns imparting their sage tidbits, I had no problem accepting the tips to schedule regular babysitters and pack the diaper bag for church the night before. These techniques seemed like logical methods to make my life easier. So I was a bit taken aback by my Grandma's frank advice—"Dear, you can expect to have 15 minutes of every hour to yourself from now on." As a girl who had always felt best when productive and efficient, I was not sure I was ready for the way time would change.

And change it did. During the first three months with a newborn the delineation of time measured by days and nights seemed odd. Days seemed to double in length as feedings every two to three hours turned night into day. The shock of this change caused my husband, John, and I quickly to forego all unnecessary tasks in order to conserve our time and energy. Tasks such as vacuuming, dusting, and cooking were deemed excessive until we were overwhelmed by dishes and dust. Having been warned about this, we had prepared by completing big projects around the house and yard before the baby was born. By the time the baby arrived, I had satisfied every item of a two-page checklist. What I was not prepared for was the challenges that come with caring for a new baby.

Not quite three days into life with a newborn I was in miserable pain from an infection that came on as a result of breastfeeding. Despite my best efforts to ward it off, the infection took hold quickly, and the excruciating pain of it rendered me in tears and quite overwhelmed. For several weeks I tried numerous nutritional approaches, poured over pamphlets on newborn feeding, and met with lactation consultants and doctors.

Still unsuccessful, I wondered how I could be failing as a parent right out of the starting gate. Though my best efforts to breastfeed were not working, I held onto the notion that it was the natural and healthy choice and a beneficial bonding experience.

However, as I held my newborn in my arms day and night, I realized I wasn't enjoying the precious firsts of my child's life. I was not savoring sweet moments such as his first exposure to warm water running down his back and the spring sunlight warming his little body into relaxation. Instead of cherishing the time I spent with this soft, tiny, new life nestled up next to me, I dreaded it.

Fortunately, I rendered many tearful prayers while the baby napped in the first challenging weeks, and I eventually began to listen for the Lord's guidance about how to proceed. I set aside the ideas imparted by books and consultants to clearly hear the Lord's will in the matter. After agonizing weeks of frustration, my mind became quiet and the spirit nudged my heart and mind to agree that it was okay to give up breastfeeding.

Thereafter we began feeding the baby exclusively from a bottle, and almost immediately I felt the heartache and frustration melt away. Now the time my son spent in my arms, chugging away on his bottle and fixing his satisfied eyes on mine, was finally enjoyable. By changing my approach I learned my first important lesson about time as a mother. My failure had not been my inability to breastfeed the baby. What I had been lacking was the ability to see that time spent pursuing a goal not meant for this season of life or for this child was hindering us from enjoying this precious time together.

After those first few months with a baby, life seemed to resume a more normal pace. However, I continued to carefully measure time in monthly increments as I followed my baby's young growth and developmental milestones. Soon I truly realized that my time was not my own anymore, and I knew I likely wouldn't have more personal time until year 18 or beyond.

Conscious that most of those years stretch out ahead of me, I have been guilty of wishing for the development of my children to go more quickly. I have anxiously dreamed of the day they will sit quietly in church. I have yearned for the time that my one–year-old will no longer try to swish his hands around in the toilet when the bathroom door is left open, eat fistfuls of dirt every time he is in the backyard, or attempt to pry open the oven to climb in. Some days much of my time is spent just redirecting his little hands and legs away from the toilet, the oven, and the dirt. On particularly rough days, I eagerly anticipate my children's little heads on their pillows fast asleep for the night.

Apparently, experienced mothers remember these years with young children, and I have marveled at the phenomenon that happens often when I pause in the grocery store's dairy section. As I turn to my cart with arms full of yogurt cups, I realize my child's cheeks are being pinched by a beaming woman, obviously older in years. Before she walks away she'll look at me and say, "Enjoy these years, dear. They go by so quickly." I nod and assume the advice is given by a mother whose children are all grown up.

One particular time this happened, one of my sons had been alternating his efforts between kicking me as we walked along the aisle, and twisting and pulling my shirt down to the point of immodesty as he lunged out of his seat. I planted him back in his seat and pulled my cart over to the milk section where I quickly began examining prices to select a gallon before he lunged again. At that point a gray-haired woman pulled her cart right next to ours, and said, "He's a beautiful boy. This time with your young ones will pass by so quickly. Enjoy it." I smiled and nodded, but inside I couldn't help but think, "Lady, your children obviously weren't as active as mine, and you've obviously forgotten how hard this time really is."

Months later I was driving home after dropping my son off at a playmate's home. I turned on a radio program and began listening as a caller told her story. She told of being pregnant with her fifth child when her oldest son suddenly died after a quick two-day illness. She talked briefly of the heartache and chaos of saying goodbye to one son as she welcomed another. However, she said, "Though I only got to spend a short time with my son, I have no regrets." She talked of spending their days having fun together. She said, "We jumped in rain puddles, dug in the dirt for worms, had picnics, and built forts. We enjoyed each and every day fully, and I'm so thankful."

Tears stung my eyes, and time spent with my children began flashing through my mind. I reflected on how quickly the years had passed since the early days when feeding my son had been so challenging. Since that time of so many emotions, several seasons had come and gone. Though parenting had become much easier since the early days, I couldn't help but wonder if I had used those seasons to enjoy the precious time I had with my children.

I immediately thought of trash truck time and felt a measure of gratitude for those moments. As I tucked the boys into bed that night, I lingered a little longer to sing all the verses of our special bedtime songs. The tenderness of these rituals reminded me of what I had learned as a new mother—that time with my children is meant to be savored, and that the Lord will help me to know how to spend that time.

Sure, I could spend my days dwelling on the frustrations of grocery shopping with children or the fact that I really do only have about 15 minutes of every hour to accomplish what I'd like to do for myself. However, I have decided I would rather heed the advice of the gray-haired women and become like the bereft mother of five. Obviously she had not whittled away time with her son fretting about her own to-do list or the inefficiencies of life with little ones. Rather, she had spent each day with her son enjoying the time with him, even if it meant crouching in the dirt searching for worms. For her son it had been worms and rain puddles. For my son it is trash trucks and playing games.

It wasn't long after hearing this radio show that I initiated a special one-on-one time with my oldest son each morning which allows us to play together without distraction. As I come back downstairs from putting the baby down for a nap, I transform from Mommy into space ranger and help Clayton defend the kitchen which becomes the galaxy we are saving from aliens. On other days I am summoned to the kitchen table to become a gingerbread girl in a game of Candy Land. Still other days I become the master architect and co-builder of a Lego hotel or mansion. No matter who we transform into for Mommy-Clayton Play Time, as we've dubbed it, we become a closer mommy and son as we enjoy spending undivided time together.

Yes, this time does go by quickly. But next time a gray-haired woman reminds me to enjoy this time, I will smile knowing that I take time each day to do just that. Besides, what other time of life will I be able to whoop and holler and jump for joy because the trash truck is coming?

Rolling with the Punches

by Bridget H. Lee

"*Please*, Rachel, no hitting!" Lately, whenever we're around other children I find myself repeating these familiar words over and over again. It amazes me how my darling, blue-eyed two-year-old suddenly transforms into a want-to-be wrestling superstar whenever other kids come into the picture. She used to know the pecking order and only push around the children that were smaller than her, but lately she's even demonstrated her physical prowess on older kids—even boys! Where am I going wrong with this little girl?

Case in point: Over Christmas break we flew back home to visit family and friends. Although Rachel sufficiently charmed her grandparents, aunts, and uncles, her more hostile side came out when I tried to show off my adorable toddler at a play date with some of my best high school friends.

First, Rachel entered the playroom and went straight for the little tent where she hid while working on a very stinky project for me to change. Oh well, every kid poops. I was sure that my friends would just be awed by how advanced she was and how well she communicated her feelings.

Smack.

Rachel chalked up her first hit of the day. I quickly went to her side and removed her from the little girl she had just pushed and explained that we do not hit. I made her say sorry and we left the room for a moment so she could calm down.

Upon re-entering the playroom she began playing nicely and I believed that our hitting episode had ended. But, she defiantly walked up to a boy twice her age and . . .

Whack.

What was she thinking? Didn't we just have a very calm conversation about how we do not hit people and hands are not for hitting? Doesn't she realize that this boy could floor her with little to no effort on his part? We left the playroom again for another talk about how hitting hurts people.

The play date continued to deteriorate even more as Rachel proceeded to hit or push all but one of the kids there. We ended up being the first people to leave. Even though we were only there for about an hour, it really felt like an eternity of trying to be a buffer between Rachel and the other children.

But her defiant attitude didn't stop there. Once we got back to my parents' home I quickly cornered my sweet husband to explain to him the antics of the tyrant we were raising. Justin peacefully started talking. "Rachel, we don't hit people. Hitting hurts. Please, no more hitting."

Even though she is very young, she usually responds quite well to an explanation like this and often repeats what we've said so we know she has understood us. Rachel exuberantly responded to my husband's counsel by exclaiming, "More hitting, YES!"

We both tried to continue and explain how we should be soft with people and share toys. But, this obviously did not make an impact when she continued to enthusiastically talk about the joys of hitting others. Rachel soon formed a one-girl picket line as she began marching around the room repeating, "Yes, hit! Hit, yes!"

Justin and I were torn between laughter and disappointment at our daughter's open defiance. If she had been raving about anything other than the delights of beating up other kids, we would have quickly pulled out our camera so that we could remember what a funny kid we were rearing. But, no such luck on the cute front, because Rachel was well on her way to becoming the captain of the preschool boxing squad. The message that hitting others hurt had obviously not made an impact that day and we were dismayed that we could not figure out a way to make this lesson stick. We realized that talking about it any more right then would be wasting our time and only adding fuel to the one-toddler party Rachel was throwing for herself. We both shrugged our shoulders and tried to steer her toward her overdue lunch.

So, I'm at my wit's end. It's truly frustrating when you cannot effectively teach your child something that can be collapsed into the succinct phrase of "we do not hit people." That message should be clearly understood and followed. At least, it seems that way to me. Rachel, obviously, disagrees.

When I used to hear people say things like, "I wish I had an instruction manual for being a parent," I would think, "I'm sure my kids will be different." Even though I knew it would be hard, I had confidence that I would be able to expertly figure out my child's unique attributes. But the reality of motherhood remains that although I do know my daughter better than anyone else, I fall embarrassingly short of understanding everything that is necessary to help her succeed. And it's not just the incident with the hitting. More often than I would like, I find myself in the dark as to how I am going to teach my little girl everything she needs to know to be the person I hope she can become.

For me, parenting has become a huge exercise in rolling with the punches. Whether with potty training, refusing to participate in activities I know she'd enjoy, or finding endless amounts of dangerous things to do in my childproofed house, Rachel really does astound me every day. Any preconceived ideas that I have had about her personality have slowly dissolved during her two years in our family. For good or bad, her unique personality has already engulfed the image of a daughter that I had been constructing for myself from the time I knew that I wanted to be a mom.

For instance, this imagined daughter would have never loved pets because I've never been a fan. However, Rachel has already developed an obsession with animals. She wants to be an animal doctor when she grows up (with the occasional exceptions of ballerina or pirate). She knows the names of not only the standard zoo animals, but many birds and insects that I do not even know. And with animal noises, she out-identifies me almost every time. Even though I never pictured myself reading books like *Armadillo Ray* a dozen times a day, I am learning to delight in how rare a child I have been given.

Although I try to roll with all of Rachel's punches, I often find that my unrealistic images of ideal children keep getting in the way. I unfairly compare Rachel to the kids around us or what I read about other children. I sometimes find myself thinking things like, "Lucie was potty-trained in one day and Rachel can communicate so much better than her. Why are we having problems with this? Why doesn't Rachel want to sing this song with the other kids? She loves to sing at our house. She should be sleeping through the night at this point. What are we doing wrong?"

It is so sad that despite the incredible child I have been given, I have a way of finding small ways that she could be better, like the other kids. It is times like these when I need to cut my daughter some slack and honestly evaluate what is reasonable behavior for Rachel and not for the other kids in her nursery class or in the pediatrician's book. I need to remind myself daily that everyone in our family is much happier when I disregard any ideas I have about how Rachel should be and enjoy the child that I actually do have.

It is because of my many parental shortcomings that I know that I have to rely on the Savior to make up for my inexperience as a mom. He is the only one that can help me roll with the punches this two-year-old often doles out. He knows what I need, and what my kids will need, to be successful in this life. He understands my weaknesses and knows how to strengthen me and sustain me through frustrations, heartache, and simply the daily bumps and bruises of life. Even though I definitely haven't mastered the art of establishing simple lessons like not hitting others, I am grateful that with his help I can. If I keep teaching her the things I know to be true and doing the best I can each day, he will help me and my family grow together and toward him.

The words of the hymn "Our Savior's Love" artfully depict how Christ will guide us through the unsure paths we see with our mortal eyes for ourselves and our children. The first verse explains:

Our Savior's love shines like the sun with perfect light.
As from above it breaks thru clouds of strife.
Lighting our way, it leads us back into his sight,
Where we may stay to share eternal life.

I love that even when I feel like I am in the dark as to how to help my child progress, I can look for his light to lead me. Little by little, he shows me the way and directs me through the significant, and often insignificant, stumbling blocks of motherhood. As Rachel surprises me with unforeseen personality quirks or behavior problems that I cannot quickly tame, if I am flexible in my responses and do not rely on my outdated image of how she should be acting, things really do start to work out in a new way that I could not have constructed for myself. The Savior and his teachings illuminate the real possibilities that my child possesses. I have already learned so much from her and know that she will continue to teach me more with Christ's light as our guide. It becomes much easier to roll with the punches when I have faith that he will steer me towards the truly important things in this life and strengthen me and my family in the process.

And who knows, maybe Rachel's mighty arm will come in handy later in life if she learns to use it wisely. Her dad doesn't think it sounds too bad to have a 16-year-old daughter who can throw a mean left hook to keep the boys away.

Accidents

by Anna J. McFadden

A matronly woman told me, "This is the easiest and best time of your life: when you have little kids you only have little problems; when you have big kids you get big problems." I tried to remember that as I chased after my three-year-old, birthday-suit-only boy peeing all over the house who laughed at me as I lunged at him in failed attempts to corral him back to the bathroom. I think that lady never potty trained a boy.

I've failed twice in the potty-training arena, and I try not to take it too personally. If there were a scoreboard, teaching potty training would rank me at the bottom. I graduated from a great university Magna Cum Laude and managed a challenging business venture with success, but a small boy with an iron will stymied my strategies and left me wondering if I was competent to be a mother.

One would think any reasonable adult could teach a small child such a straight-forward skill; hah! Four potty training books, three children's animated films, two wet-yourself dolls, and a red-handled potty, and we are still learning almost a year later.

Openly I admit that I probably started too soon and made many mistakes along the way, but I hope my nightmares of a college-age son wearing diapers are just a sub-conscious exaggeration.

The excitement of potty-training started when one of Spencer's pre-school friends was potty trained before he was two years old. It seemed she caught onto the process quickly and learned without much trouble. Her mom made it seem so simple that I began reading books to see if Spencer showed the signs that he was ready for potty training:

Can nap for several hours and maintain a dry diaper. Check.

Can communicate and follow instructions. Check.

Able to pull down his own pants. Check.

Shows interest. Check.

"Great!" I thought, "We are on our way."

My first fatal error was taking this task too seriously. I did not see things from a child's perspective and did not buy a child-size toilet or make a big deal out of this new change. I thought it would be a hassle to sanitize another toilet and have to do it several times a day, so I got a stool and borrowed a small toilet seat to go over the regular toilet. It was a padded white vinyl cover with blue knuckle-grip handles that Spencer found interesting. So that night during bath time when I noticed he was doing the cricket dance—legs crossed at the knees while pulsating up and down—I whisked him out of the tub and onto the toilet in time to assay the first potty seat. Spencer relished the praise of doing something he really had not meant to do. The next day we practiced sitting on the potty, but during one ascent onto his vinyl throne, the seat slipped and Spencer partially plunged into the toilet. He was not happy. For several days he wanted nothing to do with the bathroom at all and regarded the toilet with deep distrust. Strike one.

So, I realized, the vinyl seat cover was not going to work.

The toilet was too high and the seat slid around too much when he was trying to pull himself onto it. I swallowed my pride and resorted to buying a miniature potty, knowing it would require more sanitizing than I cared to ponder. After six months of potty-training freedom, I read another recommended book about how to potty train a child in less than a day. By this time, I felt pretty motivated to make potty training work. We had just moved, had a new baby, and settled into a routine.

Armed with a strict drilling regimen from a book, four gallons of three types of juice, four salty—and previously forbidden—snacks, and an array of shiny stickers with happy faces and "Great Job," I hoped to encourage my son to eat and drink enough to be peeing all morning. We started out with a doll that could wet after drinking and a bottle of water, and we taught the doll how to use the potty after drinking. When the doll used the potty successfully she got a treat which she passed on to my son, and when she had an accident Spencer helped her practice pulling her pants up and down, getting to the toilet on time, and cleaning up.

After twenty-four ounces of juice and an uncountable number of pretzels and cheezits later, it was Spencer's turn to pee as he had taught the doll to do. He made it the first time to our great delight, but a second round ambushed us less than five minutes later and he wet all over himself and the floor. We practiced running to the potty from all over the house to make sure we could get to the potty in time, but we had weak success. By the end of the day we had a 50 percent success rate, and the next day when we started again Spencer started running around the house screaming, "No!" as though I were after his life. The day went downhill from there. Piece by piece my sanity and patience fell away as grey hairs took their place. Strike two.

After two more days of trying to follow the plan, I realized

Spencer's determination was stronger than my desire to clean the carpet every day. I could provide treats as incentives, force clean up as punishment, and drill all day long, but if Spencer did not want to use the potty, I could not make him do it. I saw myself losing the power-struggle and realized that even a two-and-a-half-year-old can exercise his agency.

Fast forward another six months, and we come full circle to one year since the initial potty training trial. After each bowel movement Spencer would deny he needed a diaper change and would run through the house evading me or hide in cupboards to avoid detection and the inevitable diaper change. His smell always smoked him out. I offered, "If you won't let me change your diaper, you can use the potty."

"No diaper change and no potty," he declared.

Frustrated after one prolonged wrestling match in which he managed to get poop on both his legs and my arms because of his thrashing body, I issued the final threat, "If you won't let me change your diaper, you have to use the potty!"

"No diaper change and no potty," he repeated, but lay still.

Now he was calling my bluff, and I knew I had to follow through. I prayed for additional patience and an insight from Robert D. Hales reverberated through my head, "We must understand that each of our children comes with varying gifts and talents. Some . . . struggle with every decision they make. As parents, we should never let the searching and struggling of our children make us waver or lose our faith in the Lord" ("Strengthening Families: Our Sacred Duty," *Ensign*, May 1999, 32).

I venture that Elder Hales was not talking about potty-training at the time, but the idea seemed true to my problem. Spencer was struggling to figure out how to be independent, yet it still felt like I was a flawed mother. I wondered, "Should something this simple really be this hard to do? Am I really cut out for this?"

We both needed to learn how to approach an obstacle together. I realized I was approaching the situation like a business process that needed streamlining and taking all the fun and excitement out of learning a new skill while he wanted to make everything in life a game. So I changed tactics and laid out a new game plan.

I laid out all the recently-purchased treats and he was interested. Two gallons of juice, twelve juice boxes of "Freaky Fruit Punch," pretzels, chips, popcorn, and several new movies from the library all provided the needed interest to play along with Mom. I explained the "potty game" in which each successful potty experience made him a winner, celebrated with prizes.

My plan was to wake Spencer up the next morning before he went to the bathroom and accrue our first "winning experience" before an accident or diaper change. At 4:57 the next morning the baby woke up and needed to be fed, and I checked to make sure that Spencer had not woken up. Feeding the baby and wolfing down my own breakfast at the same time, I hurried in at 5:15 and found that I was too late. Spencer submitted to a ceremonious final diaper change and put on his own underwear, delighted in the prospect of drinking "Freaky Fruit Punch" and playing with Mom all day.

We placed the red, yellow, and blue miniature potty on the linoleum floor in the kitchen. The whole day seemed like a prolonged ping-pong match. I started the game with a powerful serve—irresistible juice and treats to make anyone pee (ping), but Spencer countered and scored his own point by having the first accident (pong). This time, however, the game was fun. Instead of making the accident a shameful thing, we cleaned it up, laughed it off, and tried again.

It was a personal epiphany: If you treat potty training and life like a game, the failures still occur but you're willing to try again because the process is fun. We had a jolly day in the kitchen, drawing erupting volcanoes, throwing balls and catching them, and eating lots of deliciously unhealthy snacks. When Spencer succeeded we all cheered, yet he celebrated the most at his new ability and increasing proficiency.

Yes, we still had accidents, but the tone had changed. When he asked, "Who smells?" and discovered himself as the culprit, we washed off and tried it again. In fact, we washed our hands so many times that by the end of the day we all had cracked, dry, flaky skin from the anti-bacterial soap and sanitizer. Nevertheless, we were making happy, steady progress together.

It took a couple of weeks before we could master all of the key skills, but we both learned to relax and do the best we could. Spencer still had an occasional accident when we could not find a bathroom in unfamiliar places, but I am the one who requires more practice in my motherhood training. Motherhood is one of the most difficult things I have ever undertaken in my life, and I make lots of mistakes. Qualities like long-suffering and infinite patience do not come naturally to me, but when I have "accidents" and lose my patience or temper, I can try again just like Spencer. Motherhood is a rewarding yet grueling daily marathon, but in all of our efforts we show how we "cherish and care for our children with unwavering dedication" (M. Russell Ballard, "Teach the Children," *Ensign*, May 1991, 79–80).

Potty training and motherhood is about loving and learning. We all have agency to choose how we will act or react to a situation. Every person has varying interests, strengths, and weaknesses, including both children and mothers, so what finally worked for me may not work for everyone, but in a spirit of fun and patience anything can be accomplished in the long run. Devoting all my time teaching life skills to strong-willed children who need guiding and nurturing is the price I pay to help my children know who they are, that they are loved, and that they can reach their potential.

Adopting Motherhood

by Rebecca Whitchurch Wren

After two weeks of settling into the routine of life as a mother, I took Jack to our first Mommy and Me class at the library down the road. I sat on the end of a giant semi-circle of chairs, feeling as shy and awkward as I did on the first day of Junior High. I waited and watched as other new moms filed into the room with their infants.

In my mind, I was rehearsing the answers to the questions I expected to be asked. The usual ones you'd hear in a group of new moms mingling for the first time—"How old is your baby? Is he sleeping through the night? What can he do? Does he smile yet? Roll over?"

The first round of questions would be easy. It was the questions that I suspected might follow—the ones about my labor and delivery—that caused my stomach to flutter. What could I say about that? Did I want to say anything at all? It wasn't that I was embarrassed or bothered by the birth of my son; I just didn't want to be branded or, worse, have him be branded as too different to relate to.

I listened intently as the conversations around me meandered into surprisingly detailed accounts about labor and delivery and the varying stages of the recovery process. Eventually, the woman sitting next to me leaned over and asked quietly "How old is he?" I breathed a sigh of relief at the easy first question and answered, "He's eight weeks." I smiled with all the love of any other new mother, thinking of the miracle I held in my arms, but was puzzled to be met with a hesitant expression. Incredulously, she asked, "*Eight weeks?*" and then paused before saying, "Wow! You look fantastic!"

Admittedly, it wasn't the first time I'd heard that exclamation. But it *was* the first time I didn't have the heart to simply say "thank you" and go on my merry way. This time, I laughed a little nervously and then related the story about my journey to becoming a mother.

I didn't arrive at motherhood the way I had anticipated. I had always expected that I'd get married and that, when we decided to start our family, the children would just come as we planned—no problems. But, after four years of fertility treatments and months of adoption paperwork and home study, I found myself traversing territory I'd never imagined. I was happily married, but unexpectedly childless.

It was early on a Monday morning that, when I answered the phone, I heard our caseworker tell me the news I had been praying to hear. We had been chosen for the adoption of a baby boy. Although we knew this day would come eventually, we didn't know it would come so soon. Most mothers had at least nine months to expect their new arrival. I had just three short weeks. But, as I reached out when my sweet little Jack was placed in my arms for the first time, I embraced a tiny and unexpected miracle that began my life of adopting motherhood.

I experienced new motherhood in a way that most women don't expect to—I wasn't physically recovering from the toils of childbirth, suffering from chronic sleep deprivation because of an uncomfortable pregnant body, and I didn't have to return from the hospital still wearing maternity clothes only to face a wardrobe of clothes I may never fit into again. I was a fireball of energy enjoying every second of attention that this new little person demanded—even at the midnight and 3:00 a.m. feedings.

Six months later, after I had more completely adopted motherhood and therefore actually lost some of my boundless energy, I found myself staring incredulously at the positive pregnancy test I held in my hands. Surprised and cautiously excited, I thought, "Could it really be? After all those years of failed fertility treatments, am I actually pregnant?" It was just as unexpected as Jack's quick arrival, but it was true. It was another miracle. It seemed that now I had not only adopted motherhood, I was about to be immersed in it.

Tammy, the woman I'd met that first day in the library, had become one of my dearest friends and happened to work as a labor and delivery nurse at the hospital where I was to deliver. As my pregnancy progressed and I contemplated the impending labor and delivery that I would endure, I relied on her wisdom and experience, as well as other veteran new mothers I'd become friends with, for reassurance.

I knew what it was like to *adopt* an infant, but I had only their stories on which to build my expectations for the birthing experience I would soon face. Nearly two weeks past my due date, after not-so-gracefully enduring 40 hours of slow-to-progress labor, and narrowly escaping a c-section, I held another tiny miracle in my arms, and I adopted a new kind of motherhood— the kind that comes not only with sleep deprivation, but with twice as many unexpected moments.

During the first few months following Olivia's birth, I was reminded again to embrace the attitude of expecting the unexpected. Being a mother of two infants meant no more planning to be showered, dressed, and ready for the day by a certain time in the morning. No more planning that the clothes I wore at the beginning of the day would still be clean and presentable at the end. No more tidy lists of tasks to accomplish with little checks by each item at the end of the day. I couldn't depend on anything happening the way I thought it would, and I started to learn that being prepared to be flexible was my key to survival and, more importantly, my key to fully adopting and enjoying motherhood.

My new attitude of embracing the unexpected helped make the next surprise an exciting one. Not much more than a year after Olivia's eventful birth, I found myself staring—shocked, cautiously excited, and strangely amused—at another positive pregnancy test. It was, once again, surprising. It was, once again, a miracle.

This time, as my pregnant belly became noticeable, I listened and watched as people gasped with gaping jaws and bulging eyes at the spectacle I was—awkwardly wrangling two tiny toddlers while trying to keep myself balanced and composed. Inside, I was nervous about the quick addition of a third child, but mostly I was grateful and excited for one more opportunity to adopt motherhood.

As I approached the end of this pregnancy, I was a bit more prepared mentally for the inevitable changes to motherhood that would come. I wasn't exactly certain what they'd be, but at least I knew they were coming. Regardless of my mental preparations (and meager physical ones), I was still surprised when little Anna joined our family three weeks earlier than we expected. Anna's unexpected early arrival, in many ways, helped me to internalize the biggest lesson my experiences with motherhood were trying to teach me—expecting the unexpected is the only thing I can ever really expect.

So, when my first time to host Easter Sunday dinner drew near a few months later, I knew that despite all my preparations, something surprising could happen. I've learned to expect the unexpected; but I can still be surprised at the form the unexpected takes.

I had planned the menu and carefully prepared the table—arranging a floral centerpiece, composing tiny bird's nest seating cards, and even some hand-crafted napkin rings—cleaned my home, and awaited the rare opportunity of hosting my own dinner party. As our friends arrived, Jack and Olivia welcomed them shyly with sweet and innocent smiles, and I breathed a short-lived sigh of relief that they had remembered the manners we'd rehearsed earlier.

But, soon the trouble began. Olivia, not wanting to miss a single moment of the action, refused to sit in her chair at the little table we'd set for the kids. She stayed in her seat long enough to sample a good-sized bite of ham and then came begging for a lap to sit on. Knowing that I didn't want to deal with the potential emotional meltdown that would likely ensue if I resisted Olivia's imploring, I caved and let her sit on my lap. Once she sat straddled comfortably, I noticed the bulge in her cheek. If there is anything that can shake a mother's confidence in her own cooking, it's a two-year-old who won't swallow food she doesn't like (or *thinks* she doesn't like). Olivia was holding a piece of food in her mouth (as she is prone to do) hoping that somehow, if she waited long enough, it would simply disappear.

I whispered to Olivia that she should chew and swallow her food and be careful not to spit it out. Before I even finished my pleading, she tried to swallow. Unfortunately for her (and everyone else at the table), she gagged. Her little eyes bulged, and she held her tiny hand over her mouth in a valiant attempt to keep it in—but she failed. As I realized what was about to happen, I jumped up from my chair hoping to avoid the impending disaster—but I failed.

Stepping back from the table as quickly as I could, I hurried to the bathroom to assess the clean-up situation. Her hair was wet, her hands were dripping and her pretty dress was splattered with a less-than-flattering color and fragrance. My shirt and pants were soaked and the napkin I managed to catch some of the sickness in was beginning to seep. As I began the clean-up, I had a moment to really think about what my dinner guests had just witnessed.

It was a mortifying thought, but what could I do? Only what I had done with every other little unexpected moment. I had to embrace and adopt it. I gave Olivia a bath, put her in her pajamas, and then changed my own clothes and washed up before returning to the dining room. I finished our dinner party, laughed at Olivia's embarrassing outburst with our friends and got ready for the next day of surprising moments.

For me, adopting motherhood had been just that—adopting a string of unexpected events to create a life that I thought I might never have. As I finished cleaning the dishes and tucked in my three little miracles, I prepared for middle-of-the-night wakings, diaper bursts, and kisses, hugs, and *I love you*s. After all, adopting these unexpected moments is what makes me a mother and I am grateful for each and every one.

Remembering Childhood

by Linda H. Condie

On a late spring day when I was about seven years old, my brother Steve asked me excitedly, "Hey, wanna see something really cool?"

"Yeah, what is it?" I answered with just as much excitement. Steve was a year older than I, and we spent most of our free time together.

"I can't tell you. Just get your bike and let's go."

I hopped on my bike and followed Steve to the corner. We turned left and headed up the quiet two-lane road for several blocks,.passing street after street until the houses on the right side of the road gave way to a grassy field, where a narrow ditch connected with the street. The stream in the bottom of the ditch came out from a pipe and the clear water was only a few inches deep where it exited and continued on its way.

Steve stopped by the side of the road and dropped his bike on the gravel shoulder. He lay down in the grass, hanging his head over the edge of the ditch until his face was just inches above the little brook. I followed his lead, flopping on the grass beside him and peering down into the water.

There in the shallow stream were hundreds of tiny polliwogs, swimming in a wiggling mass of gray and brown. What a great find! We watched those polliwogs for what must have been a long time, though in our childish fascination, we had no idea how late it really was.

Our fascination was suddenly interrupted when a shadow fell over us, accompanied by the sound of an idling car motor. We turned to see what was making the noise, and the first thing I saw was my mother's face in the driver's window. She wasn't smiling. Uh, oh.

Quietly she asked, "Do you two know what time it is?"

We didn't.

"It's time for dinner, and I've been looking all over the neighborhood for you. Put your bikes in the back and get in." We obeyed in silence. The only thing I remember my mother saying on the way home was, "DON'T go back there again."

She said it sternly enough that I should have remembered it, but somehow the lesson just didn't stick. I don't think it even registered. Even my mother's quiet demeanor during dinner didn't drive the message home. What my childish eyes saw then as my mother's silent displeasure, my parental eyes now recognize as the greatest fear a parent can face, that of losing her children. I'm sure she told us how we had put ourselves in great danger by going so far from home without telling anyone. Surely she told us how worried she had been when she couldn't find us, and how afraid she was that we had been kidnapped or injured—or worse—but my little brain just didn't get it.

After dinner, my brother, who apparently was just as astute as I was, suggested we go back and take a bottle with us to catch the polliwogs.

Now, you would expect some alarms to go off in my conscience at about that point, but if they did, I wasn't paying attention. That sounded like a really fun idea, so we hunted up an empty jar for each of us—even thinking so far as to get jars with lids—and rode our bikes back to the stream. We were happily and obliviously catching polliwogs when the familiar blue station wagon reappeared, Mom at the wheel, jaw set in the same expression, only deeper this time. UH, OH.

I don't remember any more about that episode. I don't remember what the punishment was for disobeying. I don't even remember recognizing that it had been wrong to go back to the stream after Mom had told us not to, although we never went back after that day. All I remember is the lesson I learned, and I don't think it was the obedience lesson my mother wanted to teach me. I learned that children do not think like adults.

Many years after that experience, I was busy with our toddler while my two older boys were supposed to be putting their toys away. When I came into their room to check on them, they were hurriedly stuffing toys under the bunk bed, apparently trying to make up time lost to a more interesting activity.

I surveyed the room and saw the results of the alternative: greasy white diaper cream artwork all over the dark brown closet doors. I felt my anger start to boil as I turned to them, ready to react to what I saw as a deliberate act of disobedience and vandalism. But, I stopped when I recognized a familiar reaction in their faces: "Uh, oh."

Just like I unknowingly disobeyed during my polliwog catching escapade, these two little boys had not been willfully malicious. I remembered how fun it had been to catch polliwogs in the stream. I'm sure they saw the diaper cream and the huge closet door canvas and thought how fun it would be to finger paint. My boys, ages 3 and 5, had simply acted on an impulse. Their frightened faces confirmed my thoughts.

I remembered my mother's calm and quiet, though firm, reaction to my own disobedience. I stifled my initial urge to vent my anger at my sons and instead explained to them why

I was unhappy with what they had done when they should have been putting their toys away. Then we worked together for several days to clean the closet doors, though we never did get all the diaper cream off. I wish I could say that from that time, I always responded correctly to my children's mistakes, but that wouldn't be true. I did, however, learn from that experience that remembering my own childhood errors could help me see my children's actions in a better perspective. Then I could handle the situation with reason, compassion, and patience instead of overreacting in panic or anger.

Several years after my stifled diaper cream reaction, I was serving in the Beehive class in the Young Women organization and feeling a little frustrated by what I perceived as very immature behavior by several of the young women. I even thought to myself, "I was never that immature." After all, my mother had often told me that I was "mature for my years."

One day, while cleaning out a closet, I came across an old journal I had long since forgotten. It contained a very detailed account of my first and second years at Young Women camp when I was the very same age as these young women. As I read my descriptions of our activities, conversations, conflicts and resolutions, as well as my own private thoughts, I was amazed. My own admissions were describing almost exactly what the young women in my class were doing, saying, and feeling.

Reading my journal helped me to see that the behavior they were exhibiting was very typical of young women at that age. That did not relieve me of the duty to teach them to love, serve, and forgive as the Savior has taught, but it did encourage me to have more patience with their efforts and struggles.

As my own children grew through the various ages of their childhood and adolescent years, I thought often of these two experiences, trying hard to remember what it was like to be their age and stifling the desire to expect them to behave as adults would.

I began to more fully appreciate Alma's sermon to the people of Gideon (Alma 7:11-12), as he explained that the Savior had suffered every kind of pain, affliction, temptation, and infirmity known to mankind. Why? So he "may know according to the flesh how to succor his people according to their infirmities." He knows what we are experiencing because he experienced it himself. He hopes that we will learn from our experiences just as he did from his.

The temptations, failures, and infirmities I experienced while growing up served the same purpose for me, if I just remembered them in the heat of the moment. When my children made mistakes, the Savior's example helped me to see their behavior with better perspective.

When I remembered that they were learning, just as I had learned, and that they would make a few mistakes in the process, I was able to command less and listen more. As a result, they were willing to talk more openly and even to listen more patiently. We learned together, and I learned to see my children more as the Lord sees each of us. Remembering who I'd been—a muddy little girl gathering polliwogs, a teenager pouring out her heart in her journal—helped me envision who my own children could become.

My Own India: Providing Home Relief through Sippy Cups and Suckers

by Brook Andreoli

"I'm a stay-at-home mom." Pause. That all-too-familiar pause that seems to inevitably follow my reply to the standard question, "What do you *do*?" The pause, a hold, as if this new acquaintance and I know that, after the standard question of my children's names and ages, our conversation will slow or turn to other topics. And so I answer, "Bronwyn, four, Davis, two, and newborn Skyler." Another pause. For me, these pauses seem to signify the identity loss I felt with the occupation change that accompanied my first child's birth. Pauses never accompanied my tales of international service or teaching immigrant English classes. Certainly, my future dreams of establishing foreign literacy programs were praised and admired, while my current dreams of nap times are not.

At times I think it would be more rewarding and perhaps more beneficial to mankind to focus my energies on building up impoverished countries, instead of taming cow licks and tempers as a stay-at-home mom. But these past few years, as a young mother, I have leaned heavily on a theme by Mother Teresa, a theme of taking care of our own homes first. Her idea was to take care of our own homes, our own children, our own neighborhoods. If we would do this there would be no "India."

"It is easy to love the people far away," Mother Teresa observed. "It is easier to give a cup of rice than to relieve the loneliness and pain of someone unloved in our own home" (*My Life for the Poor*, ed. Jose Luis Gonzalez-Balado and Janet N. Playfoot [New York: Ballantine Books, 1985], 103–104).

I have been taking care of my own India here in my own kitchen. Perhaps it is this day-by-day, hour-by-hour laying down of our lives for our children that is most difficult. This oft unnoticed, mundane work is never shelved. My friend served his mission in India several years ago. He and his companion went to Mother Teresa and asked her how they could serve. I was surprised to hear that the service she requested was the unglorious work of cleaning the toilets.

In keeping with that request, she advised, "We must not drift away from the humble works, because these are the works nobody will do. It is never too small. . . . For there are many people who can do big things, but there are very few people who will do the small things" (*Works of Love Are Works of Peace*, comp. Michael Collopy [San Francisco: Ignatius, 1996], 135).

Mother Teresa received a Nobel Prize for her work in India. I often wonder if I will ever receive the praise and visible trophies I crave for my mundane motherly works.

Sister Susan W. Tanner, the Young Women's General President, spoke of trophies in an address to the young women: "In these preparatory years, you young women spend much of your time in schools or jobs where you receive accolades, honors, awards, ribbons or trophies. When you move from that stage to young motherhood, there is a dramatic drop-off in outside commendations. Yet in no other capacity is there more opportunity to serve selflessly as Christ would do by taking care of hundreds of daily physical, emotional, and spiritual needs. You will bring the light of the gospel into your homes—not to be seen of others, but to build others—men and women of strength and light."

Sister Tanner acknowledges: "That is not an easy task. Good home life often goes unrecognized. It might be easier to 'arise and shine forth, that the light may be a standard for the *nations*' (D&C 115:5, emphasis added) rather than that your light may be a standard for *your own families*. Sometimes others don't see us doing good, sharing our light in our individual homes. It is basic human nature to desire and seek praise and attention. . . . Good works should not be done for the purpose of receiving recognition." ("I Am the Light Which Ye Shall Hold Up," *Ensign*, May 2006, 103–5.)

Charles Dickens has a character in the book *Bleak House*, a Mrs. Jellby, whose flaw he labels as "telescopic philanthropy." She is so consumed with helping a suffering tribe in a distant land that she dismisses her own bruised and dirty child who comes to her in need of comfort. Mrs. Jellby wants to make sure her good works are grandiose and visible to all. (See Charles Dickens, *Bleak House* [1985], 82-87). Maybe some of us would rather help with hurricane relief than home relief. Now both are important, but home relief is our primary and eternal responsibility.

Motherhood, at times, is a lonely battle to fight all day at home. And, well, sometimes it is a very public battle to fight, as eyebrows are raised—in sacrament meeting, at the grocery store, and on the playground. Sometimes the exalted view of motherhood is obscured by others as they watch me drag my bribed, sticky children from the store to the car—the only items purchased being the two watermelon suckers used to quiet them down the first two aisles.

Or the two suckers given at the doctor's office, ages before the shots had actually been administered at Davis' 18-month check-up. It started the moment my children were released from their car seats' restrictive straps and careened down the extended handicapped ramps. I followed, just a few steps behind. Two steps behind when they exploded into the pediatrician's office, and one step behind as Davis spied a toddler, unsteady on her feet, and bee-lined for her. I tried to catch up; I knew what was coming, but I could only watch as the toddler hit the ground as she received my son's over-exuberant bear hug. The girl's father and I both swooped down to repair the damage—perhaps more shock than anything. Davis and I received frosty glares from both parents, but Davis didn't notice as he rushed toward a dump truck. I noticed, and my continued, profuse apologies didn't even win an "It's OK" from the offended parents. I dreaded the next twenty minutes of sharing the waiting room.

After the offensive tackle, and loud apologies, all eyes were on my active children and me who in two minutes touched every surface of the waiting room. Flustered, I signed in and corralled my children back outside with the promise of running up and down the ramp. They ran up and down. Up and down. Up and down. With all that running they didn't run out of steam like I had hoped. Is this the power of oatmeal for breakfast? I only dared venture back to the waiting room when the flattened toddler had been called back.

After a painstakingly long wait we were called and I promised myself I could make it through this. They bounced on the scale and held still for their temperatures but on the way back to the examination room Bronwyn was lured by a Winnie the Pooh keyboard in Technicolor. She wrote her own diagnosis titled,

"JNASQWTYBL" before I could pull her away. Alerted to the fun, Davis tried to print out his prescription by maneuvering the matching Technicolor mouse. I dragged them away, after the waiting nurse, into our brightly decorated torture chamber.

It is in these moments that I wish to hand her my past resume and explain I really am a capable, competent woman. In this moment I know it was easier to direct a language program than to direct my children into the appropriate examination room. I no longer wished my work to be visible, I wished that I could be invisible.

I sigh as we are left in our private room—at least we won't have an audience here. I soon realize I am wrong. Like electrons my children seem to gain more and more energy each time they touch. The 8-by-8 room is giving them plenty of room for contact as they bounce off each other and every once in a while bounce out the door to examine the glass canister filled with colorful suckers atop rounded safety sticks. The promise of candy teases them and it is difficult to stay away. I promise them the treats will soon be theirs, just please come back into the room. They bounce back in.

We read every book; we crinkle every inch of the tissue-paper-covered examination table, touch every bead on the busy bead box (I try not to think about all the germs that we are contracting)—but they have seen similar toys at home and nursery and these are not nearly as interesting as anatomic ear models and multi-line office phones. As curious hands open every drawer, I wonder why child locks would be absent on a pediatrician's cabinets. I try to distract them—but Davis is drawn to the knee hammer and Bronwyn to the oily Polysporin. We put them back. I check the time. I have endured, and the children have enjoyed 75 minutes here at the office. Seventy-five minutes and we haven't seen the doctor yet. The children run out to eye the suckers again. I follow them and guiltily pull a sucker out for each—hoping to gain four quiet minutes of licking time. Davis immediately crunches his and asks for another. Defeated, I take them back to our room.

I search my memory for long-stored quotes on the nobility of motherhood when my children find a low cabinet full of infant formula cans. The cans' pastel labels advertise the essential building blocks for baby's system. My children use these cans as literal building blocks. With my help, they build towers. I think of leaving as I sense my reserves running low. I build another tower because I know we'd just have to endure this wait another day. I tell myself I can hold out—and the doctor finally enters. He eyes the towers. I hastily put the cans back and sit on a chair—I figure I will be taken more seriously without carpet burns.

Rubbing my knees, I wonder if he offers mother check-ups. Surely there can be something to measure how I'm doing. Would my kind pediatrician offer me a pocket-sized chart that showed my tidy mother percentiles? Does giving suckers before shots bring that motherhood measure down? I long to be assured that I'm not failing, that I am making a difference. I long to be praised for my inventive mothering, my wells of patience, my commitment to my cause. My pediatrician does not sense my unasked questions, or perhaps his glass canister holding mommy prizes has run low. No trophy is awarded here, but Davis is awarded with a few shots.

Finished and exhausted, I follow my electrons up the ramp to our car. Finally they are restrained in their car seats. I climb into the driver's seat and estimate that the Red Cross could have immunized ninety waiting people in the time it took to immunize the 18-month-old sitting behind me. But I carry on, my standard of princess dresses and dump trucks held high.

I carry on for the details, the priceless details that come. A detail, a memory, a moment such as this: after I put Bronwyn to bed and walk into the hallway, I hear Tim singing Christmas carols to Davis. I walk down the hall and then I pause and turn back. Where do I need to be that could be more important and memorable than this? What could be more precious than hearing my husband rock my baby boy to sleep?

I sit down in the darkened hallway to pause. To remember. To listen. I imagine it is in similar quiet moments, not in her Nobel Peace Prize acceptance, that Mother Teresa felt her work's confirmation and joy. "Love begins at home, and it is not how much we do but how much love we put into what we do" (*Works of Love Are Works of Peace*, comp. Michael Collopy [San Francisco: Ignatius Press, 1996], 195).

Soon Tim's song is obscured by a little girl's voice recounting every word in *A Very Hungry Caterpillar*, the book I had just finished reading.

This is enough. This moment means it all matters. My whole world is behind these two doors in front of me. I feel peaceful and full. As I hear Bronwyn mimic my story telling, I know I matter and my daily work matters. I know that few see my true work and perhaps most often I do not even see it myself. Yet, it is in this moment that I see. It is in this goodnight detail that I see.

Motherhood has been a time of growing up and really discovering me—rather than relying on a picture of what I thought my life would be like and a picture of what I expected I should feel like. I may not be running international literacy programs, but I am running a literacy center in my own home— a comfy spot packed with colorful, entertaining, thoughtful storybooks. Its accompanying praise comes in the form of "One more story, please" from pajama-clad lap-sitters. I may not be traveling to passport destinations, but to my children the woodsy, unexplored lots across the street are another world. More than anything my desires to study international development stemmed from a desire to help others realize their true potential. This is my moment to use my talents and time to show my children their true potential. This is my prayer—that I may do so with faith, with remembrance and vision, without tiring, with my Savior's guidance.

It takes great courage to live as the Savior: humbly serving, sharing our light with others. It takes great courage to know our mission and fulfill it daily—even hourly, sippy cup by sippy cup. Like Mother Teresa, mothers everywhere choose wisely, daily, in accord with the heavenly law of love for others. Is that not just as our Savior did as he suffered drop by drop for us? And was he often rejected or not properly recognized by so many in the world? I may not be recognized by many for my efforts, but I am certain that I am recognized by my Savior. Each of us, like our Savior, can choose to move God's plan forward as we choose to live each day of motherhood with courage.

Of Dinosaurs
and Dancing

by Tami Wilbur Chandler

My son is, among other things, a dancer. Not in a formal way, but in an ants-in-his-pants kind of way. He jumps and wiggles and bobs his head, and I think every now and then he even inadvertently throws in the Electric Slide. Though I don't understand it, I love this lack of inhibition about him. It has, however, embarrassed me on more than one occasion.

Not too long ago I decided to take him with me to a concert. We had traveled to Utah from Maryland to visit family and I took advantage of the rare timing to buy concert tickets. Since my husband had stayed in Maryland, Caleb was my date. The concert was held in the mountains of Provo Canyon, where I'd been to many concerts before, and I was as excited about introducing this new pleasure to him as I was about the concert itself. After a short climb, we arrived at the amphitheater, early enough to secure seats on the front row. I was a little nervous about how well he'd hold up all night long on hard benches-- he was only five, after all, but I resisted finding the seats closest to the exit. Caleb's arms and legs began to wiggle and his face took on an intensely focused expression that I knew signaled his excitement with this new experience. The music started and almost immediately Caleb tugged on my sleeve and asked if he could dance. Well, okay, I guess. I assumed he meant right there, in our row. But instead he hopped over the bench and ran directly in front of the stage and began moving. The singer smiled down at him, and I was embarrassed. I started to call out for him to return so I could explain about the necessity of going through life with as little notice as possible, but I caught myself. That's not his rule, it's mine. And just look at the joy on his face; I can't take that away.

I struggled with this through the first song, trying to decide if other mothers would make their children be more respectful. But just as the next song was beginning and I was regretting my decision to bring Caleb, a miracle happened: he was joined by a few more dancers. Then more and more. By the third song there were so many people dancing by the stage that I had to grab Caleb, not because of embarrassment, but because I didn't want him to get squished.

The timing was odd, but at that moment I thought of a Rodin sculpture I'd seen during my third year of college. It was a sculpture of a man, standing, with his head turned downward and his arm, bent at the elbow, outstretched toward the sky. I don't know why I was so moved by that particular sculpture among so many other works, but I was and I returned probably five or six times to the museum to study it, to sketch it, and to wonder about what Rodin was communicating.

The entire piece was magnificent, but I was particularly drawn to the hand. At the end of the man's arm, he held his hand open, as though he were letting something go, and I spent a great deal of time imagining what it might be. A bird perhaps, or maybe a heartache he'd held on to for too long; some unrealized dreams or a deep grief that he was releasing to God. Whether a bird or dream, the gesture seemed symbolic of something universally shared: the need to let go.

I learned at an early age that at some point I really had to let go of my sister's hair or I would get another time out. I learned to let go of a lost puppy that belonged to someone else, and to let go of the idea that, if I tried hard enough, it would actually be possible to fly (a particularly embarrassing low point). As I grew and became more aware of the pain in the world, the letting go got harder and more personal. Letting go of the sorrow of wrong choices, and the sting of rejection, or the people who have meant so much to me--these are all lessons I'm still learning.

As a mother, my first lesson in letting go wasn't a hard one to grasp. It occurred right about the time I was screaming that I was absolutely done with giving birth--it didn't matter that my son was only half-born. My body was trying to let go of my baby, and though I supported the general idea, I wasn't keen on the method. The tsunami of relief that washed over me when he was born is a sensation only other mothers can comprehend. Relief isn't even the right word for it. Hallelujah is closer. But I had done it; I had given my son life. And as I looked at his beautifully wrinkled face I understood that motherhood would become to me a lesson in letting go.

Two daughters have since followed Caleb, and I'm not sure I can say that my motherhood experience is quite as I'd planned. Mostly because I don't think I really had a plan. Having children was about as far as I'd envisioned. Well, that's not entirely true. Somewhere in my mind I had held onto glimpses of my future that included smiling, well-behaved children who could recite scriptures and phrases of Tennyson with equal skill. Who loved hiking and good music and laughing at old Smothers Brothers albums. Who loved to paint. It never occurred to me that I would one day bribe my children with chocolate to just PLEASE stop asking me to get the watercolors out again. Or that for months I would have to look at a volcano mural, complete with one continuous flow of "lava" on the walls, sofa and floor of our home, until I had the energy and the toxic substance necessary to remove it.

Caleb, the artist of said mural who is due to come out of time-out next week, has been obsessed with dinosaurs for well over two years. Our home has been, in no particular order, the Petrified Forest, the Smithsonian Natural History Museum, Pangaea, a prehistoric underwater habitat, and a T-Rex excavation site. He knows the difference between ornithischians and saurischians and even uses those terms. We rent documentaries at the library, or record them off TV. We re-enact scenes of dinosaur carnage, and write our own textbooks. For a while Caleb was praying about dinosaurs every night; every question he asked me related to them.

"Mom?"

"Yes, Caleb?"

"Heavenly Father doesn't like us to steal, right?"

"That's right."

"So does he get mad when oviraptors steal other dinosaurs' eggs?"

How do you answer that in a five-year-old way? I mention this, not because my son is a genius (Caleb still has trouble writing his own name), but because before I had him I didn't even know the word ornithischian existed. But I have adapted myself and adopted Caleb's interests, because while watching an hour-long documentary on the dinosaurs of Baharia is not important to me, it's very important to him.

I'm learning to let go of whatever notions existed in my mind about what my children would be like, and I'm becoming a better person because of the way my children push me to adapt and grow. I change for them in ways I couldn't have predicted: I dance though I have no rhythm, because I love to hear them laugh. I arrange playdates, though I've always hated to use the phone, because my children need friends. I do the laundry and clean bathrooms and change diapers, because . . . well, because no one else will do it, but I pretend there's some glory in that, too.

When my daughter was born with serious eye and spinal deformities I was absolutely disoriented. The first time we gave her tiny sleeping body to the waiting surgeon, we understood a new depth of what it meant to let go. But we adjusted our plans to better fit the limitations and challenges she will have (hopefully in a way that will not make her feel limited and challenged), and I make the doctor appointments, and I buy the twentieth pair of glasses to replace the ones that she broke again and we play and laugh and take each day as it comes.

My children are young right now, and the lessons in letting go that I've had are just trial runs for the really hard letting-go's in our future. I know this. I know that someday in our future my children will move away, or will experience broken hearts that aren't made better with my kiss. I know someday they will be embarrassed by me and I'll have to learn not to take it personally. But for now I will hold onto the image of my son, pointing me out as he told his friends, "Hey, that's my mom!" And I'll retrieve it when he's thirteen and makes me park two blocks away when I pick him up from baseball practice. The ways I've been asked to let go are neither unique nor as difficult as the trials other mothers endure, I know this too.

Not long after my own initiation into motherhood, I found myself again in a hospital room, one hand on my sister's hand, the other on her back, counting with her through contractions. For three hours we sat like that, breathing together through the valley of death to bring the most amazing miracle to pass. I sat with her as she held that beautiful child in her arms, and I sat with her as she placed him in the arms of another mother, tears flowing hot and free down her cheeks. My heart ached for my sister, and I was overwhelmed with the love it took for her to let go; to give this child a life she knew would be better.

As mothers we cease living our lives for ourselves. Not because we want praise, but because we love our children, and what else could we do? I don't have the time I once did to paint or hike or go to concerts. I struggle to lose those extra pounds that baby number three added, and I sometimes enjoy my time away from my kids a little more than I probably should. But, in exchange, I get the pleasure of watching my daughter taste Starlight Mint ice cream for the first time, and a son who tells me that his favorite time of day is when he crawls sleepy-eyed into bed with me to cuddle before the light creeps in our window. I get to learn, in a very small way, how my Heavenly Father feels about me.

I mother very imperfectly. In fact, I'm pretty much making it up as I go. But yesterday, as I sat outside on the porch swing, holding baby Anna on my lap while she sucked on a red ribbon she'd pulled off her head, I was happy. The day was just turning to dusk in that six o'clockish way that sends shafts of light through the trees and makes grass and clouds and children glow. Everything looks good in that light. The breeze was warm and soft, and in that moment, as I listened to Caleb and Elisabeth giggle on the trampoline, I was perfectly happy.

I don't believe that Rodin knew exactly how his sculpture would turn out when he started. He must have added or removed clay where the muscles didn't look quite right, or smoothed out the rough spots when he saw them. He probably altered his plans a little bit. Maybe that particular work of art resonated so deeply with me because I understood how much our lives are like that. As I have let go of trying to be a perfect mother, and learned to let my children grow into the best versions of themselves that they can, I've begun to realize that the sculpture that is me is only just beginning. And that most of the time the tools that sculpt me are held in little hands.

Epilogue

by Lindsay Hepworth

My sister just had her first baby.

He was long-anticipated, and he finally came after months of hormone therapies and ultimately in-vitro fertilization. Although I wasn't there when he was born, I got to talk to my sister on the phone just moments after she became a mother. Like most new mothers, she was so happy that she was crying.

We talked again a few days later after she had brought him home and was just learning the routine. She had begun to realize that her schedule was no longer dictated by the clock, but by Carson's voracious appetite. She had started to feel the effects of sleep deprivation. She had begun worrying that she was losing her before-motherhood identity as a nurse, and she was amazed that her newborn had gained so much weight in such a short time.

I listened on the other end nodding and remembering my initiation into motherhood. "Welcome to the club," I said.

It is amazing to me that women all over the world belong to this club. As mothers across all cultures we share so many of the same experiences, but we still feel so alone as we experience them for the first time. All the world seems sound asleep when we wake up to a crying newborn, but new mothers everywhere are waking up to the same cry. Words of encouragement seem to echo in the bathroom as we cheer for potty-training two-year-olds, but the same cheers erupt from bathrooms across the world.

I first realized that I belonged to a club of mothers when I was invited to my first mothers' lunch. Each month the young mothers in my married student ward would gather at one sister's house and bring pot-luck dishes to share as their children played. On the sign-up sheet that came around in Relief Society, I signed up for a main dish even though I had yet to make a from-scratch meal for my own little family.

The day arrived and I was prepared. I had chopped the veggies for the clam chowder the night before. My newborn was down for his morning nap and I was dressed. All I needed to do was make the soup, put it in the slow cooker, transfer that to the car and then put my sleeping baby in his car seat.

I assembled the soup and checked the consistency and temperature. It was perfect. While my baby was still asleep in his crib, I put on my shoes, wrapped the slow cooker in a towel and made my way to the car. It was the first time I had actually been dressed, made a meal, and gone anywhere on my own since my baby was born. I was feeling like I might actually be able to handle my new role as mom.

I guess the bulk of the slow cooker I hefted must have blocked my view of my icy walk because when I was only two steps past my door I slipped and fell. I broke my slow cooker. I splattered hot clam chowder all over my face, and I spilled the rest of my first homemade meal all over the sidewalk.

Crying, but happy that I had dropped the slow cooker and not my baby, I made my way back into the house and called the sister that was hosting the luncheon. I explained what had happened and told her I wouldn't be able to come. I was defeated.

I had failed at my first mothering excursion.

I was surprised, however, when I went to church and related my story to the other mothers who attended the luncheon. I was sure that I was the only one such a tragedy had ever happened to. After all, most mothers I knew seemed like Supermoms the moment they gave birth. Instead of dropping their jaws at my tragedy, like I had expected, the other mothers began relating similar incidents they had gone through as they first became mothers. I was amazed. I guess I wasn't so different after all. But, this could have just been a coincidence.

I decided to test the waters and mention the difficulty I had breastfeeding during the first three weeks. Similarly, other mothers piped in with their stories of mastitis and mastering the football hold. I thought I was alone in all my mothering woes. It was a huge sense of relief to realize that I wasn't.

Since that first meeting of mothering minds, I have found that I have an instant bond with each mother I meet. We're never lost for a subject of conversation. All I need to do is ask how old her children are and we're launched into relating shared experiences of grocery store fiascos and time out tendencies.

For me, this book has been a chance to record those conversations. The conversations that happen on park benches and grocery store check out lines and at kitchen tables across the world. After all, once you become a mother, wherever you are, you're a member of the club.

About the Authors

Brook Andreoli enjoys taking pictures of her children at every age, angle, and location, and helping them find prize earthworms in the garden. She is the author of "My Own India: Providing Home Relief through Sippy Cups and Suckers," and lives in Utah with her husband and three children.

Laurie Brooks, author of "Enjoy These Years, Dear, They Go By So Quickly," lives in Southern California with her husband and children. She loves taking her children to the park and eating churros with them during trips to Disneyland.

Jennifer E. Brown's least-favorite mothering activity is clipping tiny fingernails. Her favorite activities are going on nature walks with her children and reading to them at bedtime. She and her family live in Arizona. She is the author of "Everyday Pearls."

Jenny K. Call, full-time mom and part-time nurse, enjoys stamping her National Park Passport, hiking with her family, and just hanging out with her best girlfriend (daughter Elsie). She lives in Utah and is the author of "Labor and Delivery."

Melissa H. Carlos, author of "The Lord's Design," lives in New York with her husband and daughter. She relishes in singing baby songs by request, listening to her daughter's animal sounds, and being outdoors.

Melissa Baird Carpenter resides in Arizona with her husband and two children. Her little munchkins enjoy playing hide-and-seek with their mommy and listening to her read Curious George and Caillou books. She is the author of "Sane Mothers, Take a Bow."

Tami Wilbur Chandler, author of "Of Dinosaurs and Dancing," lives in Idaho with her husband and three children. She loves playing dress-up, building block castles, and running through sprinklers with her kids. She loves it even more when they do these things without her.

Allyson Condie lives in Utah in a houseful of boys. Editing this book caused the dishes to go undone for a very, very long time. That's her excuse, anyway. She is the author of "I Didn't Think This Through."

Linda Condie is a mother of five from Washington. She loves getting her hands dirty playing with her grandchildren and working in her garden. She is the author of the essay "Remembering Childhood."

Amy Ferguson Hackworth lives in Utah with her husband and two young sons. Her favorite part of motherhood is listening to her children laugh. She dreams of traveling the world and of getting a full night's sleep. She is the author of "Traveling."

Lindsay Hepworth, author of "The Hand of the Lord," lives in Las Vegas, Nevada, with her husband and soon-to-be-six-year-old little boy. She enjoys racing from the car to the front door each time they arrive at home and listening to her kindergartener read *The Cat in the Hat* to her while she cleans the bathrooms.

Bridget H. Lee, author of "Rolling with the Punches," lives in Minnesota with her husband and two children. She enjoys riding bikes and family dance parties.

Josie Lauritsen Lee lives in London, England, with her husband and two children. Her new favorite activity is watching her son make pulley systems and train tracks out of belts and shoelaces. She hates potty training. She is the author of "The Right Fit."

Anna J. McFadden, author of "Accidents Happen," lives in New York with her husband, son, and daughter. She loves storytime cuddle-fests and is an accomplished living-room blanket-tent architect.

Connie Merrell Sowards, a mother of four, lives with her family in Southern Utah. She writes to relieve stress. The worse the day, the better the journal entry! She hopes to be able to look back someday and laugh. She is the author of "Boarding the Straight and Narrow."

Elaine B. Vickers is an expert at backyard digging and basement hockey. She lives in Cedar City, Utah, with her husband and two children and is the author of "Towers."

Rebecca Whitchurch Wren lives in Wisconsin with her husband and their three energetic children. She loves pretending to be a Mommy Monster and enjoys receiving hand-picked bouquets of wilting dandelions. She is the author of "Adopting Motherhood."